LIFE WAS LIKE THAT

To Betty & Doug

Alby G. White

Dec. 2002.

LIFE WAS LIKE THAT

An Autobiographical
Reminiscence

By Alby G. White

1923 to 1946+

Copyright and all rights reserved Alby G. White. 2002.

Life Was Like That
©Alby G.White 2002.
First edition Oct.2002.

All rights reserved.
No part of this publication may be reproduced
or transmitted in any form or by any means
electronic or mechanical, including photocopy,
recording, or any information storage and
retrieval system, without permission
in writing from the copyright holder.

Topham Picturepoint
Licence No. L54801/19171.

ISBN 0-9543645-0-3

Printed by;
The Lanceni Press
Garrood Drive, Fakenham,
Norfolk. NR21 8NN.

Published by;
Alby G.White
45 Watton Road, Swaffham,
Norfolk. UK. PE37 7XA.
Allybaba@pe377xa.fsnet.co.uk

LIFE WAS LIKE THAT

PREFACE.

Whatever our future – we learn from our past.

'What was it like Grandad, when you were a boy? '
'What in particular, lad?'
'Well, everything, what was life like in those days?'

It was then that I realised just how fast, the conditions and the environment in which we live, is changing. So rapid is the speed of progress that it moves all too quickly to bury the past. In just one lifetime – my own, those things which were once everyday and normal in the formative years of my youth, have now drifted backwards in time and become history.

Looking back to my childhood before World War II, the everyday things that I grew up with and took for granted, are now only to be found in dusty attics or antique shops, museums even! The material things have at least survived, but the intangibles such as the conditions, the way of life, the experiences, and the characters of the time, survive now only in memory - in the memories of the few remaining people, like myself, who lived through those times.

How could I answer the lad, so that he could see what I have seen?

I decided therefore to record what I had experienced in the years past, before I too become a relic, a mere name on a stone, and before my memory is wiped clean like chalk from a blackboard.

This is what I told him:

2.

Addendum;

This book is not, strictly speaking, an autobiography, (for the simple reason that most of my life was mundane, and not at all unusual). Although it is autobiographical, the primary object of this book is to record the long gone characters of my youth, and the long past circumstances and incidents of that time. It is hoped that you might, in your mind's eye, look back and remember - or perhaps, simply look back to the conditions of a previous generation and thereby gain a greater appreciation of the present - by seeing a glimpse of what Life Was Like then..

1923 – 1930

I was born a bastard, well almost, but it was a situation only narrowly averted. In those days it was expected that couples wishing to *tie the knot* should obtain the permission of their prospective in-laws.

My mother's parents gave their permission readily enough, but my father's parents were a completely different *kettle of fish*. Apparently my mother's father was a sailor and he had married his second wife, my grandma, in suspicious circumstances, and that, from the viewpoint of my father's family, put them *outside the pail*. And so my paternal grandparents would not give their permission for the marriage of their son to my mum. It should be noted here that, at that time, my mother was twenty-three years of age, and my father was twenty-seven, having fought in the trenches at Ypres some six years earlier.

What a tyrannical way to carry on!

The two families lived within a few doors of each other, in a row of nondescript terraced houses, in a little back street, in the Borough of Walthamstow, on the east side of London, with the old London postcode of E.17.

But back to the nuptial situation, my parents (so I was later informed) were in love and determined not to be denied each other. So with determination and what might be called *malice aforethought*, I was deliberately conceived around Easter time in the year of grace 1923.

Now that really put the *cat amongst the pigeons*, or as my other grandma would have said, *it let the fox in the hen run*, for that was a diabolical and unthinkable situation.

An out of wedlock pregnancy was not to be permitted at any price. 'Oh Good Lord, what shall we do?' Their son and heir *had got a girl into trouble*. 'Think of the scandal, what will people say? We wont be able to face the neighbours, or our friends in church, and the Vicar – Oh Lord yes – the Vicar ! …'

In those days an unmarried mother was considered a slut and a trollop, and no self-respecting person would have anything to do with her.

The child would have to suffer the indignity of being called a Bastard, and that was a deeply offensive insult then.

So for fear of *what people might say*, sanctimonious hypocrisy was set aside and they were married - in church - in white - within the month. Every one knew of course, and some of them muttered behind their prayer books.

'Surely you knew dear, yes three months gone I hear, but she's a nice lass, good luck to them, I blame the parents.'

Every one was happy – except perhaps my paternal grandparents, who had to be content with the fact that the conventions had at least been observed.

It was a shotgun marriage to be sure, but with a difference, Mum and Dad held the shotgun. My conception was precisely what they had planned, and it worked perfectly for them. It worked quite well for me too, because if they had waited, I might have been a girl.

So there I was at the wedding I suppose, the chief guest, and the only one in the nude, not knowing, or caring, that everyone was trying to ignore me, and some were wishing that I didn't exist at all. But there I was, the reason for the enforced haste to ratify the union.

When the Vicar asked 'Will you take this woman ...etc.', I wonder if my dad responded with 'I will' or 'I already have'?

Six months later Mum was packed off to the Salvation Army Hostel for Unmarried Mothers, in the Borough of Hackney, in the east-end of London. It was there that I first saw the light of day within the sound of the Bells of Bow Church, - if the wind was in the right direction.

So it came about that I was inflicted upon this world as a London Cockney. Both I, and the year 1924, were then brand new.

1924 ... Marlon Brando and Lauren Bacall were born, and P.G.Wodehouse gave birth to Jeeves in 'The inimitable Jeeves'. The 8th.Olympic games were held in Paris. Lenin died, and Hitler was sentenced to five years in prison for a failed coup in Germany.

All such a long time ago ... In fact a lifetime and three generations past.

It seems that almost everything has changed since then, and yet so much that matters remains the same ... as I remember :

My own memory begins to serve me from the age of six, when I was attending infant's school. My early memories are in the form of isolated facts and pictures, crystal clear, but without the in-fill of individual personalities. At that early age I am sure that I was too concerned with my own self-interest to be conscious of individual characters.

My local school, at the bottom of St.Andrew's Road, was an old dilapidated Victorian building even then, and it invoked in me a feeling of foreboding and rigid authority, rather than joy.

I referred to it as *My School,* but I took no pride in it. It was yet another imposition of authority that required me to submit to it for the same period each day. As a child of that era, I was used to being told what to do and when to do it, come here, go there, sit still, be quiet, speak only when spoken to, etc. It was a discipline that we were accustomed to, and there was a security in it somehow, so that we did not see it as a hardship or a suppression of our personalities.

Compliance was all. Learning the rules was difficult, but once acquired it remained a simple and straightforward matter to be obedient when it was required. When I say that it was simple and straightforward – it was in a way – because if you didn't do as you were told, you got punished, that was simple enough to understand. At other times we could be ourselves and do our own childish things.

As I grew out of adolescence I didn't encounter that regime again until I served in the Army. But to be ordered about by morons though was quite a different matter, and a harder pill to swallow – but that is yet another story.

I can just recall my earliest school days, we sat in row upon row of tiny desks, endlessly chanting 'One two is two, - two twos are four', etc., and oh how proud I was when I could recite my 'nine times tables.'

Those tables stuck in my mind however, and for all of my life I have been grateful for them. Six sevens; seven nines; eight twelves; I have the answers in my head almost before the question is asked, it was repetitive programming of my mental computer and it worked.

My recollection of our teacher is a vague grey blob, just another figure of authority, like my grandma, whose word was law, with a persona that issued instructions but no love.

I can only remember love and warmth being dispensed by my immediate family, Mum and Dad and one of my two Grandmas. Other relations were simply people that I knew, people who were kind to me, but who didn't make me glow inside.

I clearly recall the sloping wooden floor of my classroom as it slanted down to teacher's desk, and the blackboard propped up on its wooden easel by two round pegs jammed into holes.

One little podgy girl with long red hair in plaits always sat in the front row. She was teachers pet, and would eagerly jump up to retrieve a piece of broken chalk, or to wipe the blackboard clean when asked. We called her Toad and I didn't like her.

Facing forward and neatly aligned, were four rows of tiny twin desks, I can't be certain but I have a feeling that I sat about two thirds back on one side. The ends of the desks were black painted cast iron frames, supporting the plank of wood that formed a seat, and the twin lidded box that was the desktop. They were a bit like the benches in the local park.

Eight desks to each row, and each desk had an inkwell in the middle to be shared by both pupils. Quite superfluous, as we little ones were never permitted to use ink and anyway most of the inkwells were missing or stuffed full with bits of paper.

Whenever I think of my early school days, I think of the smell, - that school always had the dank musty smell of trapped air and dampness, overlaid with a pervasive tang of carbolic.

It was so distinctive an odour that it has remained with me to this day. The closest I have got to it since was on a visit to a geriatric centre for mentally ill patients, where they sat motionless with a vacant stare in uncomprehending eyes, listening to unheeded music.

On reflection it was a surprisingly similar environment to that of my classroom.

That isolated cell of learning was walled in on all sides by dark green paint as high as we tots could reach, and above that a dull, flaking, once cream surface, was festooned with multicoloured torn paper corners, of previously exhibited works of art. All overlaid with our more recent infantile artwork.

The windows were high, too high to see out of, and gas lamps stuck out on brackets from the side walls. I never saw them lit, as we were never at school after dark. It was far removed from a happy or enjoyable environment.

Nevertheless if your crayon picture went up on the wall, especially with a gold star, you walked home on cloud nine with some stupendous and proud news to impart to mum.

When I was about seven, at the end of the school term, our class put on a little play at a school prize-giving concert. I have no idea what the play was about, but I graphically remember being dressed up in a Scots kilt and being told to stand still on a box because I was a statue.

Nerves I expect, but as I stood there before the whole school I had a desperate need to wee. Try as I might I could not contain it. I dribbled, and as the warmth ran down my leg into my borrowed socks, I didn't know whether to run off or stay put. Well - a statue can't run off, can it? I remember thinking, and I dare not move, anyway I had been told to stand dead still on pain of punishment.

I could not restrain myself, so I stood and wee'd myself on the stage, devoutly hoping that no one would notice as the box got wetter.

When the curtain fell I ran off to my classroom and getting there first I put my wet socks and knickers on the radiators to dry, and then I grabbed my shorts, and wearing only the kilt, I dashed to the toilets that were outside in the playground.

When I sheepishly came back, all hell had been let loose in my classroom, because the place stank to high heaven as the steam rose from my underpants. Teacher was furious and all my classmates were making fun of me, I just wanted to die.

I don't know exactly what happened next, maybe I died of shame, but I have never been persuaded to act on stage since.

My mum fell about laughing when I told her, so did Dad.

It was about a half-mile from home to school, and I walked both ways four times a day. Usually we walked together in groups, as other playmates waited or caught up with us.

In the mornings we ran - almost always late - but on the way home we dawdled and played marbles along the gutter or jumped onto the back of a horse and cart for a free ride.

If one of us had a farthing, there would be a big decision to make in the little sweet shop. We all packed in, giving advice on how the wealth should be spent.

The advice was always in favour of something that could be shared. But if the owner of the farthing decided to buy a gob-stopper, then to sighs of 'Ooh' the shop would quickly empty, because only if you were a really close friend would you be allowed to have a suck or two of the multicoloured golf-ball sized lollypop.

We lived in the upstairs back room of my grandparent's house. It was a simple Victorian terraced house, flat fronted, apart from a small bay window that rose from the ground to roof level. The front door was set into a recess that formed a porch just large enough to keep the rain off whilst you searched for your key.

There were two rooms and a box-room upstairs, with the front room, middle room, and kitchen downstairs. Attached to the kitchen an extension housed a scullery, and the toilet was accessed from outside in the yard.

We shared the living room-cum-kitchen, such as it was, with grandma. Grandpa died when I was about five but I have a vague recollection of a very stern man who never spoke to me directly except to shout.

He commanded the table and the house from a high backed carver chair with arms. On the back of this chair, hung a razor strop, it was long and made of leather. If anyone dared to vex him - usually me - he would strike the table with it, making a bang that scared the life out of me.

He was a tyrant who demanded obedience to his will and woe betide anyone who crossed him. When he died I am sure that no-one mourned.

I expect that Grandma was relieved to be free of him, although she carried on much in the same vein, and soon became equally disliked.

The house had a tiny front garden about three yards from house to pavement, bordered by a cast iron railing and matching gate. The back garden was larger but at fifteen yards at the most it could not be considered big. The use of the word Garden is a bit of a liberty, as it was more like a yard really because the soil was dead long since and even the grass had a struggle to survive.

The back yard ended in a high wall that connected all the gardens. It was the wall of a large furniture factory owned by a gentleman I knew as 'Old Ercollani'. The factory moved some years afterwards to a new site beside the river Lee in Lee Bridge Road.

I think the same company later produced the famous Ercol range of furniture, but I could be wrong there. I do know that we used a lot of his scrap wood to make crude toys, and to light our fires.

In those days every room, even a tiny bedroom, had its own fireplace. The nearest we ever came to a resemblance of *central 'eating*, would be a sandwich on the stairs. The existence of a fireplace however did not imply warmth, as we could only afford to light the one fire in the main living room downstairs. To warrant a fire in a bedroom it had to be insisted upon by a Doctor, and then only after the incumbent had already been covered in the family's sparse collection of overcoats etc.

The cast iron mouths of the fireplaces had a piece of plywood cut to fit the opening, and these were covered with wallpaper or a piece of matching curtain material.

Only the downstairs front room fireplace stood any chance of ever containing a fire, and then only if it was Christmas, or a family party. Otherwise it was perpetually concealed behind a folding brass fireguard.

Coal was supplied as small nuts, or in cheaper large lumps that had to be broken into manageable pieces with the coal-hammer, it was a fearsome instrument with a square flat on one side and a spike on the other. It was the universal household tool, used to repair the garden fence or to break up the winter ice.

Some of the posh houses had a coal-hole just outside the front door, where the coal was tipped down a chute into the cellar. We didn't have a cellar then, and coal was kept in the cupboard under the stairs in the back living room.

That cupboard used to terrify me, as Grandma would shut me in there in the dark if she thought I had been naughty. If mum and dad were out and grandma was baby sitting, then I would often be shut in there to keep me out of the way, or to contain me while she went to the corner shop.

I suppose she thought that if I were safely shut in, then I wouldn't be able to get up to any mischief. And so I sat there **stock-still** on the coal with just a sack under my bottom for what seemed like hours sometimes. Any movement was likely to cause an avalanche of coal, and that in turn would certainly make me dirty, resulting in even more punishment, so I sat quite still. It was dark and I could just see out into the room through a crack in the boarded wall.

10

Like a mouse in its hole, I watched the cat as it jumped onto granny's chair and curled up in comfort, and I envied the cat its freedom.

I watched the steam rise from the black kettle over on the stove. Slowly I realised that I wanted to go to the loo. 'I can wait a bit, perhaps she will be back soon' I remember thinking. But she wasn't and I had to unbutton my shorts and pee on the coal.

It was dark before she came back and let me out, she undid the latch and just walked away. - not a word, not even a kindly 'Out you come you rascal' If I had done something wrong I would have expected to be treated harshly, but I hadn't. Granny always succeeded in making me feel unwanted.

Several days later when that coal reached the fire, the smell was awful and I was glad because I got my own back in a way. I am pleased to say that the cat got the blame, as it was usually his fault anyway.

When the coal-man came he had to carry the coal sack along the narrow hallway, make a tight turn into the living room and tip the coal into the cupboard. Granny would follow in his footsteps 'Tut-tut'ing all the way if he wiped the coal bag along the wallpaper, but she usually managed to remove the marks by rubbing them with a piece of bread.

The Baker got a *short shift* too if he dared to leave a loaf that wasn't crisp, fresh, and *'today's bake'*.

In those days if someone did something wrong at their place of work in a factory, or if they arrived late, they were sent home without pay. Hence the expression of getting a short shift, meaning getting into trouble and being *told off*, (told to clock off).

Trader's roundsmen regularly delivered the basic necessities of life. They could be relied upon to deliver, whatever the weather. True, it was their livelihood but it was also a matter of pride with them. Milk of course, and bread were delivered daily, the Fishmonger called once a week, as did the Coal-man, and the Butcher's boy delivered on his bicycle if the order was anything larger than a pound of mincemeat.

The Greengrocer called every other day, and many of the other costermongers would call *'on the off-chance'*. Many times I had to run after his cart because Mum took too long finding enough change for two pounds of spuds. I would stand in my long shorts, at the back of his cart as he clattered and banged the brass weights into the pan scales.

If I had forgotten to bring a bag I had to carry the spuds back in my cap, or in the rolled up front of my jumper.

Sometimes, but not often, I might be given a bruised apple or an overripe banana, but sadly not this time. Perhaps if I had bought four pounds ...?

Mechanical transport, other than the occasional bicycle, was virtually unknown in our neighbourhood. Traders used a horse and cart, and everyone else walked. Small goods were moved in a wheelbarrow, or in a baby's old pram converted for the purpose. Larger items like bits of furniture, or the odd piano required the loan of a costermonger's barrow and the help of a neighbour.

Daily deliveries were vitally necessary then, because shopping for heavy items was nearly impossible, and perishable food could not be stored for more than a day or two. We kids spent a lot of our time running errands. We ran to the shops for mum, for grandma, for the neighbours who didn't have kids of their own, and if we were given a farthing for our trouble we ran back to the shops for ourselves.

The streets at that time were a hubbub of activity during the day; with tradesmen and costermongers coming and going, the women standing gossiping at gateways, children playing. All overlaid with the cries of chimney sweeps, or rag and bone men, hawking for business, while an old barrel organ could often be heard playing in the next street.

People tended to live their lives more outdoors then. Street-doors were usually left wide open, and neighbours would *pop in and out* with a friendly 'Coo-ee it's only me' as they walked in. Only if the door had been *pulled too* did they wait on the doormat to be invited further.

In consequence people socialised and formed close communities. There were few family secrets that remained secrets for long due to gossiping, but, *by the same token*, everyone was ready to lend a helping hand whenever needed, often without being asked and always without payment. Social services were provided by your friends and neighbours. Whenever a neighbour was in dire need, the hat went round and a penny or two from each household made all the difference between survival and deprivation. Sometimes a bunch of flowers from a back garden, or a bundle of rhubarb, or a cabbage from an allotment, replaced the ill-afforded penny.

If mum was ill, then one neighbour would offer to do the washing, another did the ironing, and someone else made sure that a meal was cooked, and so on. If old folks needed a job done, then one or more of the men attended to it without fuss or payment.

People willingly cared for each other - that's the point.

Grandma came to rule the house and my parents with a rod of iron as Granddad had done before her. Grandma hardly ever spoke to my mum, except perhaps to criticise or give orders, and Dad was never forgiven for his sinful lapse. So there was always an atmosphere at home. At that age I didn't know what it was called but I know that I felt unhappy and vulnerable whenever Grandma was around.

She was a large imposing lady, large in stature with a stern face and a big bosom. I remember her as always wearing a long dark dress, which had long sleeves buttoned tightly at the wrists, with a high collar clipped round her neck by a huge broach. Her shoes reached up beyond her ankle, and were tied with long black laces that formed a ladder from top to toe.

Both feet had bunions on the big toes but I never saw her in slippers The whole ensemble was topped off with her dark hair tied in a bun sitting over each ear. She was a rather sour and self-righteous person as I recall. In some perverse way I think she blamed me for the debacle over my parent's marriage. She always called me Boy, never by my name. I don't recall that she ever gave me a cuddle or a kind word, and I don't think that she ever laughed. Not much in her life to laugh at, I suppose.

The obvious resentment of the presence of our family in her house must have been partially instrumental in drawing Mother and me closer together. We were allies, and I am sure that we conspired in my childish way to *put one over* on Grandma. Poor Dad had to play the role of mediator and keep the peace as he walked on eggshells most of the time. There was probably shouting and squabbles sometimes when nerves got frayed, but I was too young to remember any of what was said. Just as well perhaps, as my Mum never knowingly lost an altercation. She was not the type of person to start a row, but a *right tartar* once one got started, so I expect that she usually won the day.

I last saw the inside of that house when I was seven, but I retain a vivid and detailed picture of the living room. I can see it in my mind even now. The only light that filtered into the room came through one sash window, about three feet wide. On the outside, the window was blinkered, on one side by the wall of our scullery, and on the other by the wall next door. Therefore daylight was never able to venture very far into the living room at all. Certainly never sunbeams, as I am sure that if it they had so dared, Grandma would have pulled the curtains for fear of fading something.

Those long narrow terraced houses were always short of sunlight in the middle rooms, and as the middle room was always the living room, life was lived in a dim and dull environment with little cheer. The only opening to the outside world was the narrow sash window, and since this was mostly kept tightly shut and the stove burnt more than its fair share of oxygen, it was stuffy and airless too.

The large cast iron stove had an oven set into the side of it. The fire was always lit as it was the only means of cooking, and a large black kettle hung on a hook over the stove. I can hardly remember a time, when it was not there hissing in puffs like a witch's black cat. (A gas stove came much later)

The one exception was late on a Friday night, when the fire was allowed to die down. Saturday morning it was cleaned out early and mum had to make it shine with a tin of Zebo Blacklead polish.

'Come on boy,' Grandma Called 'get on with it.' It was my job to clean the rust marks from the iron fender with Emery paper.

I knelt on the rug and started work on the fender top, rubbing away with worn out scraps of Emery paper, to remove the stains of the last week, until the steel shone a dull grey.

I can still feel her presence, as I did then, with her critical eyes watching over my shoulder ready to correct and scold my endeavours if I missed a bit. I don't suppose that I did a very good job of it at that age, but it established the fact that I was expected to help around the house as well as run errands.

High over the fireplace there was a mantle-shelf, well out of my reach where odd things entitled 'Not for little boys' were stored. I climbed on a chair once but I couldn't see anything at all mysterious, only two brass candlesticks, a rusty pair of cutters for trimming candle-wicks, a snuffer and a box of Swan Vestas matches in the tray of another tin candlestick.

Next to a blue pot holding the stubs of three pencils, there was a jam jar that contained paper tapers, but I knew about those, as I had to tear up strips of old paper and fold them length-wise to make the tapers. These were used to light things from the fire and to save on the use of matches. But search as I might I couldn't find anything exciting or wicked that had to be kept from me.

A scalloped skirt of green velvet adorned the mantle-shelf, the bottom edge trimmed with once gold tassels, and the top edge securely nailed to the wooden shelf with countless brass headed tacks.

Two large bronze statues of Greek gods with raised spears adorned the cast iron hearth, and the whole thing was protected from potential vandals like me, by a huge brass rimmed, wire fireguard hooked to the wall. Always - but always - there was at least one towel or an item of clothing hanging over the fireguard and breathing steam. Sometimes the smell of scorched cloth would bring Grandma storming into the room berating the nearest person for not moving the cloth away in time.

'Do you want to set the place alight? - I can't be everywhere at once.' - etc. etc.

On the floor in front of the fireguard there was a multicoloured rug made from strips of cloth tied into a backing of sackcloth. It was called a 'Clippy-mat', or a 'Proggy' depending on which part of England you come from. Granny had made it years ago. It got beaten, on the clothesline in the yard, every Saturday morning when the fire was cleaned. Many a time I have wished that I could do the same thing to grandma.

Four square in the centre of the room stood a wooden topped table, the bare top worn into ridges of grain from years of scrubbing. This reverend surface was the very heart of the house. Everything happened here, from baking, ironing, and dressmaking, to eating and reading the Bible. But before the Bible touched the table, the Sunday best cloth of dark red chenille would be laid, taking great care to ensure that the fringe was even all round.

Most days after tea, the tablecloth would be replaced by the red cover, and the aspidistra would be placed exactly in the centre on a lace doily. This ancient plant was the only other living thing that could tolerate sharing the room with us - apart from the cat.

The only other furniture in the room was Granny's rocking chair piled high with embroidered cushions, and four upright high backed dining chairs. Plus of course the china cabinet that crouched in one corner and protected Granny's collection of Toby jugs and Victorian china, behind its glass walls.

The picture emerges of a cramped pokey little room shared by three adults and one child, with little or no comfort apart from warmth. With only hard chairs to sit on, hard linoleum on the floor, and a constant fear of invoking Grandma's wrath, it was a miserable environment especially when it was cold or raining. Therefore whenever the weather permitted, we sat out in the back yard, or found other things to do out of doors.

Dad had a rickety old deck chair that he liked to relax in whenever he could. He kept it hanging on a nail in the outside loo when not in use. Mum used it in the daytime when Dad was at work, but she rarely had the time to spare.

It could have been very cosy indoors; it was just the presence of Grandma that made it cold and unfriendly. It was nice enough when just Mum and I shared it, hard chairs or not.

One day when Grandma was out and Mum was busy ironing, I was upstairs for some reason when I noticed that the door to Granny's room was open, so gently and with a feeling of guilt, I crept in. My memory took a series of snapshots that I can see even now. I saw an iron bedstead with brass knobs on the corners, a chest-of-drawers, a wash-hand-stand, and a big chair by the bed.

As I moved on shaking legs, towards the big chair, I had a feeling that it was not normal. It had two seats for a start, and as I lifted the top one to
look under it I nearly dropped it. To my surprise I discovered a hole and a chamber pot beneath it. I had found my first Commode.

Granny didn't have a potty under her bed - she had one in a chair, just like outside in the loo, what a good idea. Gently I lowered the lid and turned away. I gave the wash-hand-stand a passing glance as mum had one of those in her room. So moving to the chest-of-drawers I started to open a drawer when the smell of mothballs made me cough. I shut the drawer quickly, and then noticed a cupboard built into the recess beside the fireplace. Before I could investigate this, a call from Mum -

'Where are you Albert' made me scuttle out of the room in a flash.

'Coming Mum' I called back as I hurried down the stairs to more familiar surroundings.

But we must linger a while at the wash-hand-stand. As I said the house had no bathroom of any kind, and during the day we washed our hands and faces at the sink in the kitchen. Friday's we had a bath, and in between the grownups washed their private bits in their bedroom at the wash-hand-stand. This was a polished wooden two tier table, sometimes with the top shelf covered in tiles. On this stood a bowl and a large water jug, with a dish for a bar of soap. Underneath on the bottom shelf stood a white enamelled pail with a lid.

Ablutions went as follows; Water from the jug into the bowl, usually cold, wash all over with a flannel, dirty water emptied into the bucket. Take the bucket and jug down to the kitchen in the morning - empty one and refill the other - take them back. What a palaver. So that is why Mum or Dad would spend half an hour in the scullery, with the door bolted. I never knew at the time.

The best days for an *up and under* wash were Mondays, Tuesdays and Saturdays when there was at least a chance of finding some hot water still in the copper.

Monday was washday, rain or shine, and that meant lighting another fire under the 'Copper' to boil the water for washing. In the scullery out back, the water boiler - known as the Copper - was a solid brick construction built into a corner. There was an opening at the bottom in which a fire had to be lit, and set into the top of the structure was a large copper container about two feet in diameter and the same deep. (2 feet = 60 cm.)

This copper lining had a hemispherical base and there was no drain tap, so it had to be emptied with a smaller half round bailing bowl on a wooden handle. A crude wooden lid, fitted into the top, kept some of the heat in and the cat out.

This brick copper was the only method available for boiling clothes, and for heating water for the tin bath that hung on a nail in the back yard when not in use. The house had no bathroom of any kind; just a cupboard sized toilet outside in the yard. This outhouse was variously known as the Loo, the Bog, the Karsie, or the Icebox, depending on the time of year. Sometimes it was referred to as 'Dads retreat'. When we had company, it was always referred to as the Toilet for some reason.

At that time there was a shampoo known as Amarmi (the spelling may be wrong) and an advertising slogan stated, 'Friday night is Amarmi night'. It was also bath night in our household and that meant lighting the copper fire around tea time. Late in the evening, the tin bath would be brought into the living room and laboriously filled with water from the copper by means of a bucket. It had to be emptied in the same way until it was capable of being carried - with water slopping from end to end - into the back yard.

The whole family took turns to bathe. Me first - then I would be packed off to bed in clean pyjamas. Then Mum and Dad, while Grandma sat on a stool out in the scullery, close to the warmth of the copper. On fine days she would shut herself, loudly grumbling, in the front room.

'Come on you two, how much longer?' I could here her shout from upstairs as I waited for Mum to tuck me in, with her wet hair smelling nice and shampoo fresh.

Then the bath was partly emptied and refreshed with hot water for Grandma to have her ablutions after my parents had gone upstairs.

How do I know all this? - I crept downstairs once to have a peek through the gap in the door. I saw the back of my mum sitting in the bath and Dad kneeling by the side of the bath gently washing her. He had no clothes on. I ran back upstairs feeling very naughty and a little guilty.

But I digress ... Back to washday Monday: Granny scrubbed her washing on the scrubbing board with a bar of Sunlight or Lifeboy Soap, this hard yellow soap was sold in 2.inch x 2.inch x 3.inch blocks. Granny's board was made of wood, but corrugated metal ones were later used by Skiffle Groups.

I can see her now; standing at a huge porcelain sink, known as a butler's sink, and now coming back into fashion. The legs of the board stood in the sink and the top of it wedged under granny's ample bosom. With the front of her dress protected by a sackcloth apron, the washing would be rubbed vigorously up and down against the ribbed face of the scrubbing board, and periodically scrubbed with the hard soap. With the worst of the dirt thus loosened, the washing was thrown into the copper for at least half an hour *on the boil*, and even that was not a simple operation, as there were no adjustments that could be made in a hurry.

The fire was kept alight with a constant heat to keep the water boiling, and if there were too many clothes or too much water in the boiler, then it boiled over and that had to be avoided at all costs. If hot water were to boil over onto the hot bricks it would instantly turn to steam, that could crack the bricks and ruin the copper, so it mustn't be allowed to happen.

On the other hand if there was not enough water because it had been allowed to boil dry, then the clothes would be damaged and adding cold water would *take it off the boil*. Not a job for little boys I am glad to say.

The boiling clothes would be poked and prodded with the copper stick for the required time, before they were returned to the sink for a *good old rinsing*. The wet clothes were dragged steaming, on the copper stick, across the scullery from copper to sink, thus adding considerably to the water on the floor, and scaring hell out of the cat that had come to watch the proceedings.

'Get out of my way boy, find something useful to do and stop getting under my feet.'

She was probably right, but for me the clouds had come out again.

Something red got into the boil wash once and poor Dad's Sunday shirt came out pink.

'I can't wear a pink shirt' said dad in dismay.

'It's not pink, it's salmon,' mum tried to convince him.

'What's salmon?' I asked, because I hadn't the faintest idea of what salmon was, but I don't remember getting an answer.

After the soap had been rinsed out in the sink, the washing moved on to the tender mercies of the mangle. I had to help to fold the sheets, which were then passed through the wooden rollers of the mangle.

The mangle was a huge cast iron affair with two wooden rollers about 20cm. in diameter, and half a metre wide. These were driven by cast-iron cogwheels, driven in turn by a large wheel with a handle.

When I became big enough I had to turn this handle, and it took all of my weight to move it sometimes depending upon the folded thickness of the clothes going through, and the pressure of the spring on the top.

The water thus squeezed out, used to drip down and wet my legs since the wooden drip tray always leaked and missed the bucket.

Water slopped onto the floor but it didn't matter because the floor was covered with red tiles and surplus water drained out through a hole in the
wall in the far corner and so into the yard. When I say the floor was covered - It had been once, but many of the tiles where broken and some were missing. The gaps left little square puddles to be avoided until eventually the heat from the copper fire dried them out.

Mum soaked her washing in Sylvan soap flakes, but Granny had no time for any of that *new fangled stuff,* I wonder what she would have said about washing machines, and biological powders? As for bottles of fabric softener - a scent card smelling of 'Phul Nana' was probably the closest that her flannel drawers ever came to a fragrant smell, except for mothballs that is. - Stiff, starchy, and smelling of mothballs, that sums up Grandma White.

I don't think I ever knew her first name, and I don't ever recall it being used. Dad called her Mother, and Mum always referred to her as Grandma White, - at least in my hearing.

As it rained more often than not - *Monday, Washday, Rainday* - the washing had to be dried around the fireplace. - A word here about that stove - in working class houses the fireplace stove was, to the household, as an altar is to a church. It was the hub, everything was connected to it, heating, drying, cooking, boiling water, making toast, and we all sat around facing it in the evenings almost in reverence

So before the freshly washed offerings could be exposed to this icon, they had to be clean and neatly folded. Sheets, blankets, table cloths, -

'Come here Boy, give a hand. - No not that way, you do left hand over right - now you've got them twisted, pay attention do.'

Is it any wonder that I hated winter washdays with a passion. The house filled with damp air, and wet clothes hung from every conceivable hook. Everyone hated it since there were four people shut into a tiny room, with the rain lashing at the window, and a hot humid stiflingly muggy air surrounding everyone and everything. The rest of the house was, as I said, icy cold so it was not prudent to escape into another room, we just had to put up with it. I can remember drawing patterns in the steam that had condensed on the inside of the window. Why the washing wasn't postponed to the next dry day, I shall never understand, but it never was.

The awful memory of washday in the rain, comes flooding back whenever I am reminded of Robin Starch that was used on collars and cuffs, and when ironed it produced a stiff shiny finish. Also Dolly Blue Whitener has the same effect, this was a block of blue dye with a wooden peg in the middle of it, encased in a piece of muslin.

A piece of string would be tied to the peg and the dye dangled into the washing tub for the required length of time. The blue dye counteracted the ageing yellowness of the fabrics and made them look whiter.

I was often sent to the corner shop early on a Monday morning before school, to obtain these essential commodities. If mum's quick rummage through her purse didn't result in sufficient coinage, then instead of a trip to the shop, I would be sent along the road to my other grandma with the usual plea.

I ran happily to see Nanna as it was always a pleasant experience.

' Hello Nanna - Mum says, please can she have a dip of your Dolly, because we have run out again.'

'So Have I ducks, here's tuppence, be a luv and run and get a new one.'

I would have been happy to do anything for her, I would have run all the way to Southend if she had asked me. She always made me glow inside, and I loved her. So off to the corner shop I ran and came back with the Dolly Blue clutched in my hand.

'Take it to your mum first poppet, I'll collect it later. Give us a kiss then, Bye for now love.'

Then back home I would go feeling that the world was a good place to be in after all.

Monday evenings meant a row of three or four flat irons heating in turn on the stove, and the pungent smell of hot damp clothes permeated the house even on dry days.

Irons then were made of solid cast iron with a piece of gas pipe for a handle. Every housewife had her own favourite iron cloth. This was usually made of several layers of towelling encased in a coarse linen bag. Unless newly made it was always permanently folded with scorch marks and burn holes on the underside.

Pressing was done with a wet cloth, and so even more hot damp steam rose into the air. Sometimes Mum would sprinkle some diluted rose water or eau-de-Cologne on the clothes before she ironed them.

Speaking of fragrant smells – Scent cards were used a lot by women in those days when perfume was too expensive to contemplate. They were about the size of a modern credit card, but made of a soft cardboard and impregnated with scent. The cards were printed for advertising, or for fund raising, and were sold for a few coppers. Ladies kept them in their handbag, or amongst their underwear in a drawer.

Popular fragrances were Phul Nana, Lavender, and Passion Flower.

Dad's Church bought a few hundred and sold them for a penny each, to raise funds. I helped him to count and pack them once, and I suffered in school the next day because I 'smelled like a sissy girl'.

I used to pass a little sweet shop on my way to school, where small treats could be bought for a farthing (960 to the £.) Two ounces of sweets cost a half-penny or as we cockney kids said a 'apenny.

For the record - two ounces equals 56.8 grams and one half-penny is equal to 0·2 pence. That is half a kilo for less than two decimal pence.

In those days an 'apenny would also buy a bottle of pop as long as you took a bottle back. Pop bottles were half pint size and they had a glass marble secured in the neck. Drinks were made to order; a measure of your chosen flavour, fill up with water, and then a blast of CO_2 from a cylinder under the counter completed the job. The pressure of the gas pushed the marble up against a rubber ring and so sealed the bottle. You had to push the marble down with one finger to be able to drink it, and then a good shake made the gas pressure seal it again.

Blackcurrant was the worst as it stained your shirt, and that could get you into terrible trouble from Mum.

Sometimes, rich people, like grownups, bought pop in big bottles. My favourite, whenever I could get any, was R.White's Cream Soda. I wasn't keen on Ginger Beer at all.

The lady who ran the sweet shop was a tiny little person who could hardly see over the counter. She had several boxes on the floor behind the counter, and she would stand on these at strategic points where she needed to be a bit taller. We used to delight in getting her to walk from one end of the counter to the other, as she would bob up and down like a little hamster as she passed from box to box. Her shoes would knock on the box as she stood on them, so 'up-knock-knock-down, up-knock-knock-down,' would set us off into peals of laughter.

She was a pleasant little body, red haired with large round eyes, a pointed nose, and a voice that chirruped like a cockatoo. If you went in when the shop was empty, you might find her working in the back room, and she would pop out all agitated and flustered, as if caught in the act of doing something naughty.

I think - in her case - chance would have been a fine thing.

One time, between Christmas and the date of my birthday, a friend of Dad's came to visit us – Frank, I think his name was - anyway, he took me to the sweet shop. He said that I could choose anything that I liked.

'It's for your Birthday Albert lad, what would you like, Eh?'

'Can I have some chocolate toffees please?' I said, not really believing that he meant it.

Then, when the precious toffees were clutched in my hand, he said, 'Keep going, choose something else lad.' And so it went on, and I remember going home with an armful of paper bags, each of which must have cost a penny. He probably spent a shilling on me and I was convinced that he was a millionaire.

It made such an impression on me that I can vividly remember the feeling as I walked home, with the pockets of my knee length shorts stuffed with sweets, and the remainder held tightly in the rolled up front of my jumper. I had a spanking new, crisp copy of The Beano as well, but Uncle Frank carried that for me.

When I gave the Walnut Whip to Mum she cried but I didn't know why.

Sadly I can't recall what he looked like. I can just remember that Uncle Frank and Auntie Dolly were family friends, and that he worked on railway steam engines and they lived in Swindon.

I once bought a packet of 'Fisherman's Friend' because I saw a man buy some. I cried because I hated the taste and I had wasted all of my pocket money for the whole week. Dad said that I had learned a lesson, but I have no idea what it was, except that Dad ate the 'Fisherman's Friends'.

A totter used to come round the streets about once a week, pushing an old and rickety costermonger's handcart, it had a buckled wheel. Just why I should remember that I don't know, but the picture is stuck in my mind of him wobbling along the road calling out *'any ol' jars or bottles.'* He would collect jam jars and bottles of all kinds and we kids could get a windmill on a stick in exchange for a few jars, or a sherbet dip for a couple of two-pound jars.

We could never afford to buy jam by the two pounds. Mum always got the one pound size and then only plum jam *'cos it was the cheapest*. I once amassed a collection of six jars because I found some in an old shed, and I got a whole toffee apple for those. I know my mum pinched a big lump off of the toffee rim. 'To make sure it's O.K.' she said, but I wasn't convinced of the necessity.

We kids were always on the look out for empty beer bottles because they were as good as money. A pint bottle returned to the off-licence was worth a halfpenny and no questions asked. Some boys used to jump over the back wall of the off-licence into the yard where the bottles were stored. A selection of bottles would then be passed back over the wall. Eventually these would be taken round to the shop and exchanged for money.

But I wouldn't do that would I ? ... Well no, but I did get a penny for being lookout once.

The totter who collected jam jars was an old chap (everyone was old to me then, in truth he was probably half my present age.) He had a white moustache and he wore a battered bowler hat.

In writing this I am astonished that these details remain in my mind so clearly. They are like snapshots in an old album; I can turn a mental page, see it and write about it. The mind I suppose is very impressionable at that young age and many such images have stayed with me.

I find that the memories of my youth, are more vivid than those of my middle years, and present day recollections tend to fade quicker now with advancing age - Now where was I?

I used to enjoy the walking bands the best of all the personalities that roamed the streets. These were made up of groups of World War One veterans playing various instruments. There was always a big drum and a trumpet, and sometimes a man with a banjo or a penny-whistle. They were accompanied by at least one chap covered in medals, probably with only one leg, or a missing arm, who proffered a tin to collect a few coins. I can distinctly remember a penny-whistle player who was blind. His mate, with a tambourine, led him along with one hand linked into his arm.

Everyone gave a coin or two, even if they couldn't afford it, because they knew what these poor devils had been through, and they were grateful.

We kids knew nothing of this, or of the sacrifices that they had made in the trenches, but we delighted in marching behind them and trying to keep in step with the music.

Costermongers with various wares came round the streets, and they all seemed to scratch a living of sorts. They were an integral part of London life then. In rain, sunshine, fog, snow and ice, the streets were where they earned their living. Street vending, - from the paperboy (man) standing on the corner, to the milkman, the greengrocer, the baker, coalman or whoever else, - it was a way of life.

They were good to us kids, and the greengrocer for instance would often give us a couple of grapes or an apple that was on the turn. His street cry of *'Apples an' sound pears - all fresh'* always started us kids running to his barrow *on the scrounge*.

The rag and bone man had a horse and cart to collect his 'tottings' and he paid cash, so he was always popular, and he would take almost anything. He preferred old prams and bikes - washing machines and refrigerators hadn't been invented - but he would take an old tin bath or a dustbin with a hole in it, an enamelled bucket, or a rusty iron bedstead.

His old horse would plod along slower than a funeral, while he walked alongside the cart ringing a hand bell and crying *'Any old rags, bones, or lumber.'* At a whistle from him the horse would stop while he loaded his gear and paid the punter a few coppers, then off it would go again at a steady plod. A reliable, automatic, horse brain motivated, transport system, driven by hay and a kind word.

Speaking of tin baths with a hole in them, reminds me that in those days you could buy a repair kit for a penny. It consisted of two cork washers, inside two metal washers, with a screw and nut through the centre. With a cork and a metal washer positioned each side of the hole, and a screw tightened to clamp them together, a bath tub with a hole could be made to serve a further term. But if the hole was in the bottom - take care not to sit on the screw!

Dad did it once - you should have heard him yell. The neighbours did !

I can still see Mum laughing as she stuck a strip of plaster and cotton wool across his bottom. Dad yelled again when she dabbed some iodine on it.

I particularly remember one day when I was about six and a half, going on seven, I was sent to the corner shop for tuppence worth of fish paste for tea one Friday evening.

Fish-paste and meat-paste was sold loose from a flat earthenware dish, and the top was covered with a layer of waxy hard fat, which kept it airtight, and it was sold by the ounce. (28.4 grams.)

Anyway this particular evening Dad had just given mother the housekeeping money of two golden sovereigns. (£2) and she had no other change. So with one of these precious coins clutched in my little hand, and warnings to go straight there and back ringing in my ears, I ran to the corner shop on my errand. I tripped up the curb, fell headlong, let go of the sovereign and I watched it roll along the pavement and disappear down a drain. With my knees torn and bleeding and the palms of my hands skinned, I ran tearfully and fearfully home, dreading what might happen next.

'I fell Mum, I didn't mean to I tripped and I lost the money it rolled

down a drain and I couldn't stop it I'm sorry Mum and my knees hurt.'
All of the words tumbled out together in one long nervous breath.

Mum was very good; she didn't scold, but rather blamed herself for sending me in charge of a whole sovereign. Mum washed and dressed my wounds with lint and boracic ointment (the cure all of the day), then with my knees wrapped in clean rags, the problem of the lost wealth was passed to dad.

Dad was marvellous too, he went out into the scullery and got the bailer bowl from the copper, I thought at first that he was going to hit me with it, but he said in a calm voice;

'Come on lad, show me which drain.' and off he went.

He soon lifted the grid from the drain, and I can see him now lying full length on the road with one arm extended down the drain holding the bailer. He scooped up ladles of black smelly mud, which he sorted right there in the gutter. Eventually there was a shiny coin to reward his efforts and it proved to be a half sovereign.

'I thought you had a whole sovereign son' he said by way of a question.

'Yes I did Dad, I am certain'.

'Let's keep looking then' he replied with a broad grin on his face.
That grin cheered me up no end, because it meant that I was forgiven - no longer *in the doghouse* so to speak.

Next we found a half crown (two shillings and sixpence. 8 =£1), then – hurrah - our precious sovereign. After that, two pennies and a sixpence were added to the hoard before Dad gave up.

So leaving a nice clean drain behind us we returned home to give mum the good news, but she knew already as she had been watching anxiously from the front gate.

I never did get the fish paste. Instead the half-crown bought us a fish and chip supper from Oats's fish shop at the bottom of Higham Hill, a rare luxury. Mum got an extra half-sovereign, and I had a whole silver sixpence to myself - I was rich at last.

My father worked at Arthur Dunhill's the famous tobacco pipe manufacturer, and he used to grind and shape rosewood pipe bowls by hand, that was a skilled job and he earned reasonably good wages. Every Friday when he came home from work he always had a little treat for me. It was usually a penny bar of Nestle's milk chocolate that he obtained from the little red vending machine on the station platform.

We were never, what was known as 'well off', but we managed well enough it seemed to me. Looking back there must have been a lot of heart ache and worry for my parents but I was always shielded from it.

I had plenty of toys: Lead soldiers, train sets, and busses made of tin plate. I wish I still had them they are worth a fortune now. My favourite I think was a large box of Meccano, most of it old and well worn, but I made many weird contraptions with it. Sometimes Dad came home with a few bits and pieces to add to my collection.

Then one day he arrived home with the *piece de resistance* – an electric motor and a battery. I was *over the moon* and my little world could want for nothing more.

I decided that I would become an inventor when I grew up, I was going to invent machines - I told Mum, but she just smiled. She didn't know then how determined I could be.

My Mum's mum lived a few doors along in the same street as us, turn right out of the front door and second house from the end, and I ran along to her whenever I could find an excuse. She was a lovely lady always full of fun, loving and forgiving. I think of her as my *real Gran*. and I called her Nanna. She was the one I would always turn to for understanding and someone who would always take my part.

Just the opposite of my dad's mum that we lived with. Nanna was the source of many sayings that I recall, some rude, most not, but always funny and they make me smile even now whenever I have cause to use them.

For instance, if I were out playing in the street and kept going back indoors for a ball or something, she would say;

'Settle down boy you're in and out like a fart in a colander'.

Rude - yes, but very descriptive and to the point.

'You'll never know your luck until you tread in it'. Was yet another of her sayings. Once when I was teasing her and being a pest she said;

'Pack it in, that's as far as you go for tuppence.'

I didn't always know what she meant, but I loved her dearly.

A little ditty she taught me, went like this –
Little fly upon the wall, 'aint you got no clothes at all?
'Aint you got no shimmy shirt? Lummy 'aint you cold?
So fly off now, and do your best, to get yourself a little vest.

   Her second husband, though not my real granddad, was in the merchant navy, and so I didn't see him very often. Whenever he was home though, he kept me enthralled with his tales of adventure. Whether they were true or not was of no consequence to me, because I believed every word and he was my hero who had been to 'foreign parts'.
   He was a huge man and he often picked me up with just one hand. He delighted in roughing my face with his beard and teasing me.
   Strength, love and kindness, all in one, I adored him too.

Nanna's house, like ours was small, that meant small rooms, so we kids were encouraged to *play out* as much as possible. That meant playing out in the street. We would dash home from school, have our tea – usually bread and jam, or a teacake - and rush out to congregate in the street.

A crowd of us would play together, and sometimes we would drift off in a cloud, like migrating starlings, to play in the next street or in the local recreation ground. Perhaps we would all go off to ensure that someone spent their pocket money wisely, or visit the nearest rubbish dump to ferret for pram wheels or ball bearings, to build scooters or carts.

Once there, one kid might shout 'let's build a den'. And so, pram wheels forgotten, we would all rummage for pieces of wood or a sheet of corrugated iron. When the den was built, and it was occupied by some of us, the rest would then start a battle for possession by pelting the shelter with anything available.

Often we stayed out until it became dark, before we wandered back home in twos or threes, sometimes with torn knees or scratches but always dirty enough to be told off.

We children were totally safe from adult interference of any kind then. So what has happened to change that I wonder? What was the catalyst that eventually took away children's security?

This sadly illustrates that not everything has changed for the better.

In those days all traffic - certainly in our area - was horse drawn, and even that was *few and far between*, so that for kids playing in the street it was *as safe as houses*.

I remember one time I was playing out with a boy down the road, when his mum called him in to his tea. He asked her if I could come too and she said yes. I entered their house for the first time and I recall thinking it was rather scruffy and it had a funny smell. I found the odour unpleasant; a mixture of damp plaster, cooking and cats, all rolled into one.

His mum was very nice and I noticed her crisp floral pinafore as she gave me a cup of tea, but I was appalled to find she had given it to me in a jam jar. Our family was poor, but a jam jar? When I mentioned it to Mother later she said;

'We are very lucky dear, some families don't have a father in work, and some don't have a father at all since the war, so you must never judge people by what they posses, but by what they are'.

I have never forgotten that advice, but to be honest - I sometimes forget to apply it.

The street was our normal and natural playground. With the houses being small, the families usually large, and everyone sharing the one living room, the street was the only place that we could play. There was a recreation ground (we called it the Rec.) and a park, but they were too far away for us to use all the time, so we kids lived in the street.

If it rained we would rather sit in a doorway and play 'Five stones' than go indoors. 'Indoors' meant Mum using the kitchen table to prepare a meal, with Dad doing something else on one corner of it. The back-draught of the chimney would bring smoke into the room to add to the smoke from Dad's pipe, add to that Granny's smell of mothballs and four people in a pokey room, and you will appreciate why we preferred to *play out*.

When I was seven I had to leave the infants school and move to the junior school. - Same building, different entrance, - and we moved house at that time, because Mum was pregnant again and we were in dire need of *a place of our own* as Dad put it.

We were all certainly looking forward to being free of Grandma's rule.

I didn't know then of course that Mum was 'expecting'. I only discovered about it years later when I was also told that the expected addition to our family was a stillborn little girl.

Sadly that was not an unusual occurrence in those days when prognosis came with the birth and not before. What amazes me now, is that Mum and Dad endured all of this trauma without me ever noticing that anything was wrong. They had managed to cope with all that heartache and yet not to let any of it be transmitted to me. That takes guts and a lot of selfless love. I wish now that I had been able to give them some form of comfort at such a time. Perhaps I did, but I shall never know.

It isn't until you grow up that you realise how shielded you were as a child, from all of the concerns and problems of parents. Things like sex, and its many consequences, violence and crime, and the worry of poverty. None of these things took any part in our young lives. Without television we were never exposed to them, and therefore we were not corrupted by any of them. Only when we were old enough to understand these things were we required to cope with them.

It is my view that exposure to these ills too early in a young life, is like being exposed to a virus – the young mind is not mature enough to be able to resist the infection, and therefore it is corrupted, and it is contagious.

The corrosion of hard drugs, and the rot caused by the lack of respect, are just symptoms of contamination too early in an immature mind.

---oOo---

World War I. Memorial Service November 11th. cc 1930

1931 – 1935

Our new home was to be a flat over an oil shop in Higham Hill Road, close by the junction with St. Andrew's Road, down which I used to run to school. We arranged to move in on a Thursday afternoon when it was half day closing. Mum opened the door to the shop to be greeted by a ting from the door bell. I didn't know then just how many hundreds of times I was to hear that sound.

As I followed Mum into the shop, I was enchanted by the wonderful aroma of the place, and the Aladdin's cave atmosphere that it had. In spite of living only a quarter of a mile away, I had never been into this shop before and I was fascinated by it.

'Afternoon Mr.Galmondsway,' said Mum. 'We have arrived to take up residence, if that is convenient.'

'It is, and you are most welcome.' replied a kindly voice.

'And this is young Albert I presume.' As he spoke he lifted the flap of the counter for us to pass through. Dad, who was behind me replied with a chuckle;

'Yes indeed our son and heir, but he'll not be getting much at this rate.' They all laughed, and I wondered why I wouldn't get much hair.

'Welcome young man, I hope that we shall be friends quite soon.'

Mr Galmondsway smiled down at me as he put his hand on my shoulder with a gentle pat. For the first time in my life I felt like royalty. I was being treated with a kind of grownup respect by a stranger, and it made me feel as if I really mattered. Added to that - here I was behind the counter of a real shop as if I had every right to be there - it was a whole new world and I am sure that I grew six inches in that moment as I followed Mum up the stairs.

The only way in or out was through the shop and up the back stairs. Mr Galmondsway placed a lot of trust in us as he handed Dad a set of shop keys. His trust was well placed as we never took as much as a biscuit. I distinctly remember that we found a penny on the floor once when the shop was shut, and mother left it on top of the till.

My new school was next to my old one, except that now I was in the Juniors and was one of the big boys. Or so I thought, until the bigger boys made me realise that it was their pond, and I was still only a little fish.

The classrooms were much the same, but we had slightly larger desks, and there was only room for 48 children per class, in four rows of twin desks. I was given the job of milk-monitor. A very important job, or so I thought. I didn't realise then that I was merely a skivvy doing a job that was Teacher's responsibility.

Schools were provided with free milk for students of our age, and the milk was delivered each morning in crates. It was left in the nearest place to the school front door that the milkman could dump it. I had to *appoint* another boy to help me carry two crates to our classroom, and then I had to give out one bottle to each pupil. The bottles were one third of a pint size, with a large neck, and each had a cardboard lid in the top. In the centre of the lid a partly cut hole could be pushed out - or rather in - and into this hole a straw was inserted for drinking.

The only advantage of being milk monitor was that you occasionally, - but only very occasionally - got an extra bottle of milk if there was one left over. More often than not though, teacher took it for the staff room tea.

In those days straws were just that, *straws*, straight pieces of natural wheat or barley straw, not paper or plastic. (Plastic, what's that?) It follows then; that the straws were of different sizes, and one straw would slide inside another. We had re-invented the blowpipe!

In the junior's school we were considered grown up enough to use pen and ink. Not Biro's dear reader, but pen nibs and wet ink, in inkwells. With a little ingenuity a pen nib could be fixed to the end of a straw, like an arrowhead, and when fired it would - and did - stick into things. A brilliant weapon, because after firing, the *gun* was just an innocent straw for sucking milk.

Now you can understand why everyone wanted to sit at the back of the class. Straw darts were to be seen, stuck into our classroom ceiling, the front of teacher's desk, the blackboard, and often the backs of the necks of the kids in the front, until the threat of the cane; i.e. *six of the best*, made it too risky. But it was fun while it lasted. The school caretaker was the most upset because when he had to dislodge them from the ceiling with a broom, they fell down on him point first.

The Cane or the threat of it was very effective in keeping us kids in order, and when Teacher said

'That's enough Albert, go and fetch the stick and book.'

Order and compliance was immediately restored in the class as I slunk out of the door. It was bad enough to have to go round the whole school, knocking politely on each classroom door, because as I entered every eye fell upon me as I stood in the doorway. I said timidly and as politely and as meekly as I possibly could,

'Please Sir, have you got the Stick and Book?' It was pure humiliation, as everyone knew exactly why I was asking.

A curt NO from the teacher who was cross at being interrupted, and sniggers from the pupils who were glad not to be in my position, sent me to yet another class in my quest. As I wandered from room to room, I was forced to wonder how many strokes I would receive. Would it be two or a full half-dozen, - perhaps only two - I wasn't that bad was I? I was only talking - but then Teacher's in a bad mood. ...Oh hell!

Eventually I returned to Class with the infamous Stick and Record book, trying hard not to drop one or the other, as I tried to open the door with my free hand in which a slight tremble betrayed the anxiety I felt. This was it, how many? I wished that I had behaved myself.

Teacher took the punishment device and banged it down upon his desk, then he glowered at me, the pause seamed to last for ever.

'Now sit down and behave yourself', he demanded, and I sat - never quicker - what a relief - let off - what luck ... Phew!

The very sight of that black book and that thin cane, served to ensure a class of angels for the rest of the day. I did get two strokes on my hands once, and it hurt like hell. It didn't do any lasting damage and I made damned sure that I didn't get any more.

I wasn't converted, I just made sure that I never got caught again. The net result was that everyone, including me, behaved whenever a teacher was around, and especially in class. It was a system that worked very well. Bring back the Cane I say. It is my opinion that children actually have a psychological need for fair but firm discipline.

The oil shop I came to know intimately over the four years that we lived there, and it is a wonderland of memories for me.

Paraffin and methylated spirits were kept in large steel tanks in the back room of the shop. The tanks stood on brick piers so that the heavy brass drain taps were well clear of the floor. The contents were dispensed into measuring jugs and spilled on the floor. The drip trays overflowed and the volatile liquid soaked into the floorboards.

That same back room also stored candles and matches, bundles of firewood, and turpentine or white spirit in half pint bottles. It was a firebomb waiting to happen and we lived directly above it.

Out in the shop butter was sold from a paper lined wooden box that weighed seven pounds. The contents had to be scooped out with butter pats, deftly patted into shape on a piece of greaseproof paper. Then after weighing, it was wrapped again in another piece of clean white grocer's paper.

No neatly pre-packed, pre-weighed, regimented and refrigerated blocks then. But it did have the advantage that Mum could buy two ounces when she couldn't afford any more. Even so, those two ounces received the same meticulous care.

Sugar, oats, bran, coffee and tea, soapflakes and dried peas, currants and flour, all these commodities came from hessian sacks with their edges rolled down to the level of the remaining contents. The sacks arranged along one wall, rested on each other for support. A large scoop transferred the produce to the scales for weighing and packing into stiff blue paper bags. If the amount was small, then a square of white paper would be expertly twisted into a cone, filled, and fold sealed in the blinking of an eye. Anything that you couldn't pick up was wrapped in paper, Eggs were placed loose in a paper bag, everything else stayed as it was and shoppers provided their own carrying bags or baskets. Household dustbins didn't fill up anywhere near so quickly then.

There was a spring balance scale on the end of the counter, it had a large pointer about twelve inches long that swung like an upside-down pendulum. This was used for weighing lighter purchases, while a huge pair of pan scales, with large brass and cast-iron weights up to seven pounds each, was used for weighing potatoes etc. It was also used to weigh babies sometimes *just to oblige*.

In front of the counter, on a shelf, there were tins of biscuits and the top ones had a piece of glass fitted into the lid so that the contents could be seen. Biscuits made by Crawfords, Jacobs, Huntley and Palmers, or Gray Dunn & Co., were usually bought by the half pound in our household, and then only for Sunday tea if we had company.

But if we didn't have company to impress, we usually bought a bag of assorted broken biscuits as these were much cheaper. A half-pound equals 227 grams and we didn't get many cream ones. Mum always pinched the ginger nuts and Dad favoured the Garibaldi's. I wasn't fussy.

I can recall that a broom handle cost one penny (240 to the £.) and a cane for bad boys cost a halfpenny. I had many an *'apennywerf* on my backside in those days and probably deserved it.

One day a woman was in the shop when she asked;

'How much are those penny broomsticks?'

I said something rude, I was banned from the shop for a week, and I got a whack with the cane as well. But I honestly can't remember what I said.

Mum called me a *little devil*, and Nanna said I was a *scamp*.

Lifebuoy or Sunlight soap; sold as two bars joined together weighing a pound, cost two pence. Beechams powders, Oxo, Dolly blue, and Robin starch vied for space on the shelves in no particular order. All mixed in with Zebo, Brasso, Bournville cocoa, Kiwi shoe polish, Bovril, Ovaltine and Bemax, Vim, Oxydol, Quaker Oats, Camp coffee, Ostermilk, H.P.sauce and Pan Yan Pickle. An almost endless list of items all stored *cheek by jowl*.

But Mr.Galmondsway never ordered more than a dozen of anything, and when delivered, they went up on the shelves wherever room could be found. But never-the-less he could lay his hand on anything without even looking.

I can distinctly remember that a range of Baldwin's Pills were kept in a counter drawer, but I don't think I ever knew what they were for. To my delight I recently discovered an old handbill which advertised them and this is what they claimed to cure-

BALDWIN'S HERBAL FEMALE PILLS - Recòmmended for all disorders of the female constitution especially during the 'change of life' 6d. or One Shilling per box.

BALDWIN'S NERVOUS PILLS - Cures nervousness, irritability of temper, headache, want of strength and energy, fear, dread, neuralgia, hysteria, disturbed sleep, melancholy, insomnia, and all nerve pains and diseases. 1/1 & 2/9 per box.

That's one shilling and one penny, and two shillings and nine pence per box. It doesn't say how many pills were in a box though.

I joined the Ovaltinies, and when our programme was broadcast on the wireless we sang;
We are the Ovaltinies, little girls and boys,
Make your request we'll not refuse you,
we are here just to amuse you.
Would you like a song or story, will you share our joys?
At games and sports we're more than keen,
because we all drink Ovaltine, we're happy girls and boys.

The shelves that lined the shop contained; Paxo, Oxo, Silko, Bisto, Blanco, Rinso, Omo, Zebo, and Brasso, Shinio, Cremo, Veno's, and probably several more. I have often wondered; just what was the commercial magic in the letter 'O'?

I have reason to remember that cooking salt was sold in large loaf sized blocks for a penny, and I will tell you that story later.

White enamelled jugs were oddly priced at two shillings per pint. A two-pint jug - four shillings, half-gallon jug - eight shillings and so on. I can remember the prices because I sometimes helped to serve in the shop after school. Black iron pots with handles like a tank's gun, sold for ten bob to a pound depending on the size.

It was amazing just how much stock was packed into that little shop. Shovels to teapots, Brooms, buckets, and bones for corsets, all had a home somewhere. Stiff white shirt collars, were sold loose as that is the way that they were worn. These were held in place on the neckband of the shirt by long and short collar studs, short at the back and long at the front.

Stiff white collars made of paper were popular because they were cheap. Even more popular for the working man, was no collar at all.

In the drawers behind the counter there were packets of Whitening - for doorsteps and canvas shoes, French chalk- to make the lino slippery for party dancing, Pumice powder- to clean the sink and bath, Bee's wax – to polish the best furniture, and so on -and so on. A mixture of bee's wax and pumice powder was used to clean metalwork.

There were so many commodities, stored out of sight, and far too numerous to mention.

That emporium was hardly ever empty, as harassed housewives would pop in for the odd purchase and *put it on the slate* until Friday. Mums and married daughters, wearing their uniform of slippers and a pinny, usually with their hair in curlers under a scarf tied behind the head. Purchases would be dropped into a wickerwork basket or a bag made from a hessian sack. Small items were carried in the front pocket of the essential pinafore, like baby kangaroos, sharing space with the almost empty purse, a few hairpins and the odd hair-curler, that had fallen out.

Older babies were usually carried on the right hip with their little legs astride the hip bone. Few families could afford a pushchair as well as a pram, even though they were always second hand, so older children had to share a worn out pram along with the shopping if they were lucky enough.

Children sent on *errands* waited respectfully at the back of the shop until their elders had been served. Waiting near the sack of currants was the favourite place as it was sometimes possible to slip a few into a grubby mouth when no one was looking.

If gossip was being exchanged by the mums, then the kids were often kept waiting for quite a while, resulting in a telling off when they got home for taking too long and allegedly playing about on the way. Since we kids were never allowed to answer back, the injustice often seemed harsh and unfair, but the smart from a slap on the leg soon wore off and it was the price one had to pay for being *seen and not heard.*

It was surprising what little ears heard though, when standing unobserved at the back of the shop. We felt very grown up when we retold it all to Mum.

'Are you sure she said that, you are not making it up are you?
'No Mum I'm sure.' ...
'Well I never, who would have thought it? Dear oh dear.'

Fresh food stock included cheese, and bacon, and eggs, and potatoes. Cheese was cut with a piece of piano wire fitted with wooden handles at each end, and bacon was sliced to order on a hand-operated slicer. If any mother sat her baby on the counter whilst being served, old Mr.Galmondsway, who owned and ran the shop would relate his favourite joke;

'Please get the baby's bottom off the bacon slicer madam, as we are getting a little behind with the orders.'

He was usually the only one to laugh, but I thought it funny. I can see him now standing behind his counter, handlebar moustache, white shirt, black tie, waistcoat sheltering his watch and chain and always a starched white apron sat on his portly tummy. His shirt cuffs were held up clear of his hands, by a pair of silver-plated armbands, positioned just above his elbows. When on the food counter, he mostly wore Over-sleeves that protected his shirt from wrist to elbow. His deep but gentle voice confirmed the impression of a very kindly and genial man, which in fact he was.

COOKED MEATS

	per lb		per lb
Pressed and Cooked Beef, Veal, Mutton, Lamb	3 0½	Liver Sausage	1 8
do. do. (sliced)	3 6	Cured Eyepieces, cooked or uncooked	8
Pressed and Cooked Pork	3 6	Meat Roll or Galantine	1 5
do. do. (sliced)	4 0	Brawn, including Potted Head	1 8
Pressed Ox and Calf Tongues	5 8	Haggis	1 10
do. do. (sliced)	6 4	Uncooked Cured Tongues, Ox & Calf (Short cut)	2 6
Pressed & Cooked Other Tongues	4 10½	,, ,, ,, All Others	2 1
do. do. (sliced)	5 4	,, ,, ,, Chaps	1 7
Pork Sausages	2 2½	,, ,, ,, Cooked ,, ,, bone in	2 4
Sausage Meat	1 11	,, ,, ,, ,, ,, ,, boneless	2 8
Slicing Sausage	1 11	Cooked Tripe	1 4
Beef Sausages	1 6½	Cooked Pigs' Feet	1 6
Sausage Meat	1 2	Cowheel	8
Slicing Sausage	1 3½	Dripping	1 4½
Luncheon Sausage, Breakfast Sausage or Polony	1 5		

There were no computers then to simplify his job, just pen and ledgers to keep control of his stock, order book and cash flow. Travelling salesmen called regularly to remind him to stock up on their particular line and to take his verbal order for more.

'Six more of those, another half a stone of two inch nails, three white-enamelled buckets with lids and wooden handles, three galvanised without, two boxes of candles, and a dozen gas mantles'.

Then the Heinz man would come in and wait politely at the back of the shop until the customers had been served, before he turned his order book to a fresh page. A dozen small beans, six oxtail soups, and six tomato. ...

And so it went, cash on the nail and seldom out of stock.

He did however have an assistant who came in to serve every afternoon, in order that Mr.Galmondsway could spend some time on his books. He was a crotchety old devil, that assistant. He always wore a brown shop coat, and one afternoon I saw him with a slice of dried tomato firmly planted in the centre of his tie.

'What are you laughing at you scallywag, What is it eh?'

But I didn't tell him, and he thought that the customers were being friendly when they smiled at him. Except that is for old Mrs.Wilkins, she took one look at him, snorted, and flounced out of the shop. Perhaps she thought that it might dislodge and fall into her sliced brawn. I busied myself tidying up the bundles of firewood, as I had been told to do.

'What's up with everybody today? They either smile at me or have a face like a wet week. I don't know what's come over everyone. Must be the weather I suppose'.

I always considered him to be ancient because he hobbled about with a permanent stoop. He leaned on the counter so often that I was sure that he would fall over if the counter were to suddenly disappear.

It was funny to watch him trying to serve butter, as he hadn't got a clue how to use butter pats. It was like watching a cross eyed man use chopsticks. The last straw was when a lump of best butter finished in the sawdust on the floor. I can hear Mr.Galmondsway's kindly voice saying;

'Don't try it again Fred, call me next time eh?' I went for the shovel to clear it up, but when I got back the cat had got there first. So I carried it *out back* and let him finish it.

Poor old Fred, he didn't take kindly to children for some reason so I tried to keep out of his way whenever I was helping in the shop. Well I thought that I was helping, most of the time I expect I was just tolerated.

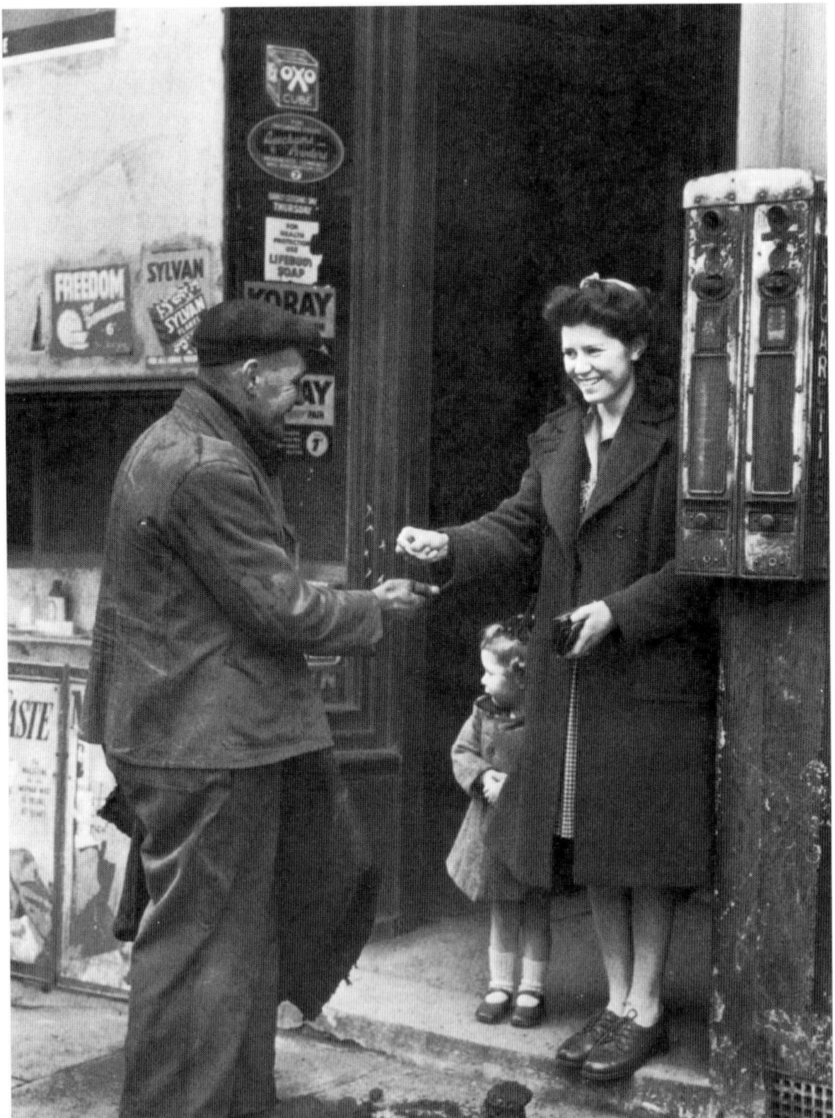
OXO
CUBE
LIFEBUOY
SOAP
KORAY
FREEDOM
SYLVAN

Next door to the oil shop there was a paper shop, I say was, there still is - at least up to a few months ago. This cramped little shop used to sell sweets, tobacco, and any grocery or provisions, which the oil shop didn't stock. Most packets of cigarettes contained small cards, which I collected and they were issued in sets to encourage the continued use of the same brand. At the start of a new series, small albums were given away free for the cards to be stuck into.

We boys used to keep ours loose because we competed for them at playtime. One boy with a fistful of cards would chose to be banker, and he would build a tent of two or three cards, free standing by leaning against each other. Then the punters would try to knock down the tent by flicking their own cards at it from a set distance. If you knocked it down you claimed all the cards for yourself, but if you missed you lost the cards you had thrown.

Card flicking became very skilful and very accurate with practice and a slight bend in the card made it more aerodynamic. At certain times of the year this pastime occupied all of our playtimes in the school yard. When the bell went, there was a mad scramble to collect your cards before someone else did and then to get into line before being marched back into class.

Sometime we collected complete sets by scrounging, winning, or exchange - we called them *Swops*. There were famous footballer and cricketer sets to collect, and sets of trains, boats, army regimental badges, aeroplanes, and a great many others. One brand, which I cannot recall, issued small squares of silk with flowers embroidered on them. They were really beautifully made. They were only issued in packets of twenty cigarettes because the silk squares were that size. I had saved a complete set once in a special album, but now sadly lost because they would be worth a lot of money now. I have still got one however, set into a small silver frame - a gift from a friend who read the draft of this book.

The Cigarette brand names that I can call to mind were Player's Navy Cut, Player's Weights, Wills Wild Woodbines, Black Cat, Greys, Kensitas with four for your friends, Clipper, Churchman's No.1, Capstan, Wills Star, du Maurier, De Reszke, Park Drive, Passing Cloud, Three Bells, Senior Service, Gold Flake, Craven A, and Silk Cut.

Most of these were just sixpence for ten, (two and a half decimal pence) or eleven and a halfpence for twenty. Machines took a shilling and had a halfpenny change pushed into the cellophane wrapper.

Just think -Twenty cigarettes for One Shilling = 400 'ciggies' for a One Pound note ?

Except Churchman's No.1 priced at 20 for 1s 2d. and State Express 555 which were claimed to be hand made and sold at 2 shillings for 25. For the record – I couldn't remember all of these, or the prices, so I researched them for interest's sake.

I do however remember about sweets. Almost all sweets were sold loose from rows of large glass jars and every purchase had to be weighed and tipped into a paper bag. Unwrapped sweets like acid drops and jellies were usually two pence for a quarter pound, (4 ounces, or 114 grams.) but separately wrapped sweets like Sharps Blue Bird toffees or Cadbury's assorted Chocolates cost four-pence or sixpence a quarter pound. The most I could usually afford of anything was one ounce for an 'apenny. Usually my limit was a stick of liquorice for a farthing. Displays of chocolate that were left on the shop counter had DUMMY printed across the front. I wonder why?

Sometimes I bought a comic from the paper shop but as these cost two-pence each I couldn't do it often. A local second hand book shop would buy used comics for a halfpenny each, and sell them for a penny, sometimes three for two-pence if they were well worn. They also exchanged one for two and that was how I got most of mine, or by 'one for one' swops with friends at school.

I used to like browsing in that shop and looking at the books that I couldn't afford to buy.

'Can I tidy up your books please mister?'

If the shop wasn't too busy the man usually let me because I had often done it before. I called them all books, but they were only piles of old magazines, and I was allowed to read through them as I neatly restacked them.

It was there that I saw my first picture of a nude woman, and I was so excited that I didn't notice the name of the book. Although I went back many times I couldn't find it again and it was a long time before I found another.

One day a boy brought to school a copy of 'Health and Efficiency' magazine and that had pictures of nude ladies in it. Cor' bli'me that was summink t' see – not arf'.

One counter in that shop was stacked with piles of comics with names familiar to every child; Comic Cuts, Beano, Chips, Dandy, The Eagle, Radio Fun, The Wizard and The Rainbow.

'Come on lad, you're supposed to be tidying them not reading them all.' This was said with a chuckle because he didn't mind really, and I did tidy them - eventually.

Later I used to read boy's papers like The Boy's Own, The Triumph, The Adventure and Champion, Hotspur, The Magnet and The Rover. These are some I can recall but there were many others. My particular favourite was The Meccano Magazine but that cost sixpence because it was published monthly, and I had to rely on Dad getting a copy of that for me.

The paper shop also sold large sheets of printed cartridge paper that were designed to be cut out and glued together to make boats, or doll's houses, or fortresses for lead soldiers, or small model aeroplanes.

The cost of these has given them their title, and to this day they are referred to as; *a penny plain, or tuppence coloured*. Cutting and pasting these kept me occupied for hours, especially as I only ever bought the plain ones and I had to colour them first. Mum used to help me and we spent hours together painting and sticking, when Dad was down at his church meetings.

Children's pastimes seemed to have a season, I don't know even now what governed it, but there was conker time, marble time, whipping top time, spinning tops, hoop and stick time, grottoes, and of course Guy Fawkes time. Guys and conkers were date related but I don't know about the others.

Whipping tops were quite different from spinning tops; whipping tops were made of wood in the shape of a mushroom with a long stem. The stem had a blunt point at the bottom and this ended with a round-headed nail to protect the point on which it spun. A small whip with a twelve inch long stick handle, secured to a leather bootlace thong about two feet long, was employed to lash the top so that it spun ever faster.

Sometimes over-enthusiasm would cause the whip to lock around the top, and send it flying, often through a window. They were banned from the school playground for obvious reasons.

Whipping tops were always painted with red and blue bands around the sides, and a coloured ring on the top. Why? I have no idea. At whipping top time, both top and whip could be bought in sweet shops for tuppence. I got mine by swopping a dozen of my multi-coloured marbles with a kid at school.

Spinning tops on the other hand were pear shaped, short and stubby, with straight sides that tapered down to a point and ended with a short steel peg. These were usually made of hardwood. A piece of string would be carefully wound around the top starting at the peg, with each turn neatly laid against the previous one until the string reached the domed top. With the free end of the string wrapped around a finger, a deft throw and flick of the wrist would set the top spinning.

We competed in the playground for the longest spinning throw and paid the winner with faggy cards or marbles, whichever was the prevailing currency.

I had a hoop. It was a bicycle wheel rim without spokes, and I ran along the street with it keeping it running by whacking it with a stick every so often. Later I learned to hold the stick pointing to the ground and to run the wheel rim along the stick. In that way it was possible to push the wheel and steer it at the same time. As I ran, the hoop clattered and bounced in front of me. There was a rusty patch that kept flickering below me, and the faster I ran the faster it flickered. I had a job to control it as it bounced up the curb. 'Burr - burr' I went as I drove my car to even higher speeds . . . then CRASH as it hit a tree and spun into the road.

Luckily my make believe car wasn't damaged, so off we went again clattering along the pavement. I didn't know then that I was maintaining a tradition, children have been trundling hoops with a stick since the sixteenth century.

Guy Fawkes' enterprise a few hundred years later in 1605, was remembered on the fifth of November, and so we made a guy of course, and sat him in a borrowed pram or barrow, then we put him in a busy part of the street and pleaded with passers by;

*'A penny for the Guy please. Please give a penny.
If you haven't got a penny, a ha'penny will do,
If you haven't got a ha'penny, then God bless you.'*

That was the polite version, but I am sure there were many rude variants to the last four words if our pleas were ignored. We always collected enough money for a large box of fireworks, plus several packets of sparklers, and boxes of coloured matches.

Grottoes - as we called them - were another ruse to scrounge a few coppers. We would decorate a paving stone close to the wall, first with coloured chalk, then to this we added small flowers and moss, coloured beads, small stones and anything else that we could lay our hands on, to make pictures, faces or patterns. Some were really good.

Outside the railway station on a Friday evening, was a good place, and well worth the ten minute walk from home. Having built our Grotto we would sit beside it and await a thrown copper or two as the workers came home with their wages. I usually gave my mum most of what I got.

Things were good for a while and we were happy enjoying life. There was just Mum, Dad and me. We enjoyed the freedom that *our own place* gave us. Mum blossomed and Dad was happy caring for his family in his own way. But it was too good to last for long because things started to change.

Poor old dad lost his job when the economic depression of the 30s started to take hold and affect everyone. Dad was mortified at being out of work and 'on the dole' for a while, and *times got hard.*

I was only eight, going on nine, and couldn't help much. Money gradually became even scarcer, we scrimped and scraped and went without. In the shop downstairs things were *put on the slate* and settled with the dole money on Thursdays. The old chap in the shop was very good, and he *carried the slate* for a lot of his regulars until they could pay a bit off it.

Everybody *felt the pinch,* workers lost their jobs or were on half time, traders suffered because people had less cash available, and costermongers had to spend far longer on the streets to make a meagre living. I think the only people to benefit were the pawnbrokers.

Dad was lucky, he managed to get a job sweeping the local roads. He brought home less than three pounds a week, but it kept the wolf from the door and he was glad for the work.

Records show that there were well over three million people out of work in 1933 and that is a much higher proportion of the population unemployed than it would be now.

I remember noticing Dad's shoes one Sunday morning just after he had cleaned them, and they told the story of both Dad and the conditions of the time. They were clean, shining brightly, worn down at the heel, and with a knot in the broken laces.

Dad's sister, Auntie Daisy, was a dressmaker and she worked from home *running up* garments for a local factory. She would collect say, four dozen dresses in pre-cut pieces on a Monday morning, sew them together, and return forty-eight saleable dresses the following Monday. So in order to *make ends meet* Mum started to do the same, but she had to sub-contract as it were, from Auntie Daisy. That meant that in addition to all the other things she had to do, she would spend most afternoons on her Singer sewing machine. I would often come home from school to find her little legs going nineteen to the dozen on the treadle of the Singer.

'Can't stop luv.' she would say, 'Got to get these finished, get yourself a slice of bread and jam, but don't go away because I want you to take these round to Daisy's in about an hour's time.' Then as an afterthought -

'Make me a cuppa, there's a dear, I'm parched.'

Aunt Daisy lived in Billet Road so it wasn't far, about half a mile each way, so I took the work in a wheel barrow that Dad had made using an apple box mounted on a pair of old pram wheels.

Sometimes I might take her a cabbage, or some tomatoes, from Dad's allotment, and bring back last week's copy of 'Women's Own' for Mum. Price 3d every Friday.

Mum taught me how to use the sewing machine, and sometimes I helped her by sewing the belts for the dresses. It was the fashion then for ladies dresses to have a cloth belt made of a matching material, and they were simple to sew, hence that became my special job. Sometime later I bought a second hand motor from a stall in the market when I was about twelve, and I converted mum's machine to run on electricity. It was my birthday present for her and she was *over the moon* with it, because it saved her poor old legs and she could work faster.

Dad was a very conscientious worker, so that before long his ability was recognised and he was promoted to the position of foreman. With the extra money that this provided, and with mum's sewing, conditions at home improved a little, and I suppose that we managed better than most during the Depression years.

Because Dad was now a foreman he had to supervise the other road-sweepers, therefore the Local Council gave him a bicycle. This was a heavy-framed sturdy machine made by Riley, and when Dad came home at lunchtime - we called it Dinnertime then because a working family had Breakfast, Dinner, and Tea. So dinner was the main midday meal. Anyway, whenever I could, I used to borrow his bike and ride it up and down the road. I couldn't reach the pedals and so I would sit astride the crossbar and ride it that way. One day the front wheel hit the curb, I slid along the crossbar and was brought to an abrupt halt by the handle bar stem meeting my crotch. That was the first time that I learned the lesson of just how painful that can be, and I didn't ride Dad's bike again until I was much older and could sit on the saddle.

One Christmas time when I was about ten, Dad came home with a cardboard box full of wires and small light bulbs, and a large battery. He hung these lights over the Christmas tree and after a lot of fiddling with the bulbs he eventually got them to light. So far - so good. But then he decided to connect in a switch. But he couldn't decide whether to cut a wire or connect it across the two.

Now I knew more about electricity at the age of ten, than dear old Dad ever did. I insisted that he should cut the wire and connect the switch to the ends. Perhaps the idea of a ten year old knowing best rankled with him, but anyway he did it the other way. He switched the switch and the lights went out.

'There you are I told you.' he said, very pleased with himself.

'Of course it did Dad,' I said, 'You've shorted it out.'

But he wouldn't listen. The battery was a big one, like a car battery, and before long there was a smell of burning as the wires from the battery to the switch glowed red hot. This was quickly followed by sparks and pieces of red hot wire falling onto the lino and burning lines in it. At this point Mum stepped in and insisted that the whole contraption be removed forthwith before he set the house ablaze. So much for science, we went back to candles on the Christmas tree.

In spite of all that we did to boost our income, we still remained poor, and as fast as we earned a *bob or two,* the conditions gradually got worse. And so we went *one bob forward and one bob back.* It was not only us, but the same for everyone that we knew. It began to show; in well-worn boots, and dilapidated clothes, in going without, and making do. I think that the old people were hit the hardest, especially the pensioners who lived alone on a pittance. Some poor souls even resorted to begging and a few were forced to steal to feed their children. Those who were least able to cope with less, were hit the hardest by the economic depression of the thirties We didn't know it then, but all this learning to make do on even less than normal, was to stand us in good stead years later when the war came.

My father was a good and honest man who lived for his family and his Baptist Church. He was a Church Deacon and loved his religion, but although I had been brought up to attend Sunday school, I only went through the motions and never really took the dogma into my heart.
I couldn't take seriously all that we were told at Sunday school, to me they were just fairy stories. I didn't believe in miracles and even at that age I couldn't accept the idea of omnipotent beings living way up in the clouds.
The teachings of Christianity as a way of life - fine, but I simply could not accept the doctrine. I still can't.
Nevertheless on Sundays we dressed up in our best clothes and off we went to the little church at the bottom of Higham Hill, close by the Walthamstow Avenue football ground. The Church's pride and joy was an ancient organ, and sometimes it was my turn to pump the huge wooden handle to provide the air pressure. To be honest, it was dad's turn, but he always passed it on to me on some pretext. If I didn't pump hard enough, the organ sighed like a run down gramophone and everyone would stare at me with scorn. How dare I spoil the hymns? - ME! Spoil the hymns? - you should have heard the singing - and the organist wasn't much better. The old stalwarts knew the words of the hymns by heart and didn't need to read the hymnbook. That gave them time to keep an eye on me in case I should flag. Fortunately I only had to do it once every six weeks or so.

Sunday meeting at the Baptist church was called the P.S.A. or 'Pleasant Sunday Afternoon'. That makes me smile now, but to dad it was all very serious. He would stand up in his best Sunday collar and tie to read the lesson, and he always made sure that I had a penny for the collection plate, however hard up we were. I confess that when the plate came round, I found it very hard to let go of that penny.

I went on a church outing to the seaside in a charabanc when I was ten, and I have a faded photograph of me playing on the sands with my wife to be of many years later. A charabanc was an early form of single decked bus and was known to Cockneys as a 'Sharra'. -
'Cum on Gel, git on the sharra or yorl miss it! ... Mind yer 'ed.'
Every time that we went on a church outing, my dad always got *togged up* in the same clothes, flannel trousers, white canvas shoes, a suit jacket and a white shirt worn open necked, with the collar of the shirt folded outside the jacket. I suppose that was his version of casual clothes, or as near as he could get from his limited wardrobe.
After church, Sunday tea, and always dead on time a street pedlar came round with a coster's barrow, and he would always call '*Cockles, Mussels, Luv-er-ly Whelks*'. Dad always had a plateful of Winkles (sea snails) and I used to remove the lids for him with a hatpin. I couldn't understand how he could eat the horrid things, I still don't, and I never eat molluscs, even now.
Do I hear you ask 'What is a hatpin'? - No? - well I'll tell you anyway: It is like a darning needle only about six inches long, and it has a large bead at the blunt end. This pin was thrust into a ladies hat, through her hair bun, and out of the other side. Thus it kept the hat in place even in very high winds. The hatpin was an essential part of every woman's paraphernalia. The bead on the pinhead was often replaced with quite elaborate decorations, and collectors of such unusual objects, prize the numerous variations that have survived - But back to Sunday tea-time ; ...

I can remember being *told off* once for 'wasting good food' because I put some jam on a piece of stale cake.
'Jam is for bread, cake is cake and think yourself lucky' my dad said.
Sunday was special because we usually had cake at teatime. At closing time on Saturdays we used to buy a large bagful of leftover cakes from

the baker a few doors along. He would let us have them for a few pennies because freezers were unheard of, and he couldn't store them until Monday.

At the time of writing, that shop is still a bakers at No.190.

Mum made stale bread into a bread pudding - dark brown and solid with lots of currants, like cold Christmas pudding, and I loved that. I think it is an East London speciality because I haven't seen it anywhere else.

Stale cake - not that we ever kept it long enough to go stale - the baker did though and he reconstituted it and put it between two layers of pastry. It was called a *slab of Nelson*, (Nelson's eye - pie) and it was delicious. A lot of the cakes that we enjoyed then seem to have survived. Eccles cakes, rock cakes, coconut cakes called cheesecakes, (I never did know why!), jam tarts, bath buns, Chelsea buns, and mincemeat slices, to name but a few. While others like grandma's parkin, and lardy cakes, seem to have gone out of fashion. We even had crumpets sometimes, bought not half an hour earlier from the muffin man, who came round the streets with a bell, carrying a tray of muffins and crumpets on his head. These we toasted by the fire, and ate them with margarine or jam, but never both. We had a three pronged fork made from stiff wire, this had a long handle that could be extended when the fire was particularly hot. I was glad of it because toasting was usually my job, and with only short trousers to protect my legs, they soon became bright red. No electric toasters then, no electricity, so no fire - no toast.

It must have been about this time when the workmen came and fitted the new fangled 'automatic gas lights' to my real Gran's house. That is my Mum's mum, she was a small lively old lady with a wicked sense of humour. As I told you, she always took my side if I fell out with my mum, by reminding her of what she was like when she was just a little shaver, like me. (ie; A shaving off the old block, - your parents).

I have just realised that I referred to *the new fangled automatic gaslights*, but the word *fangled* is not in the dictionary. In fact I cannot find any reference to it. But it is a word much used in my childhood to describe any new or seemingly unnecessary innovation, something that we can do without - never had it - why do we need it?

'Nanna' was a typical 'wire-haired terrier' type of Cockney lady, small in body but big in heart, tough as old boots but as soft as a pillow, nevertheless she would stand no truck from anyone, she was my stereotype - My Nanna'. Domestic electric lighting had begun to take hold, and so the Gas Company installed, free of charge, - otherwise Nanna wouldn't have had it done, - a device they called 'Automatic lighting'. This consisted of a large brass lever on the wall, which moved wires, which in turn moved the remote gas tap. The wires ran up the wall, over two pulleys, along the ceiling to the gas light in the centre. The trouble was that a pilot light had to be left burning next to the gas-mantle, and that used far too much gas. So Nanna used to turn the gas on at the wall, and then stand on a chair to light the lamp with a match or a taper just as she had always done.

So much for innovation, but at least she could turn it off from the wall when she took her candle up to bed.

The oil-shop already had the *new fangled electricity* connected, but only to two rooms upstairs and the shop. The outside of the shop was still lit by two large black gas lamps hanging on brackets. The gas tap for these had a brass bar fitted across it, and two hanging chains with rings on the bottom. This made it possible to turn them on and off from the ground by means of a long hooked pole.

The first electric supply was 200 volts and D.C. (That is Direct Current not Alternating Current, A.C. as it is now.) I now know just how unmanageable and dangerous that was. I find it incredible that it was ever installed, but it was. It was changed over to an A.C. supply, almost immediately afterwards however, and the voltage became 230.

After the installation of electricity, the iniquitous back room of the shop had some questionably safe equipment fitted, that was screwed to the front of a large polished wood panel that hung on the wall. This was used to re-charge small two volt batteries for 'the wireless'. They were called accumulators in those days. This panel carried open knife switches, meters, and transformers that would not look out of place in a Frankenstein laboratory. The thought of that suspect electrical equipment and frequent sparks from the switches, being cheek by jowl with all the other contents of the room - makes my blood run cold. It was little consolation to know that the fire station was only a quarter of a mile away at the top of Higham Hill, in Forest Road. If that back room had caught alight, it could have started the second Fire of London. And the stairs, the only way out of the upstairs flat, led down straight into it.

Behind this fire bomb there was a smaller room that was used as a store room.

'Pop out to the store, will you Albert and fetch another four tins of baked beans, and a large Ostermilk for Mrs Watson. Then check the rest of the stock, will you? No more than three of anything on the shelves remember, we can't afford the space now.'

And so I would clamber over piles of half empty boxes to find what was needed. I had to stack the empty boxes in the passageway so that Mr Galmondsway would know that it was time to reorder. When he had made a note, I was allowed to burn the empty boxes in the back yard. I enjoyed that.

Wireless sets at that time had to have no less than three different batteries to run them. The two-volt accumulator heated up the valve heaters to a cherry red. The mysterious bias battery provided a series of connections for various voltages up to nine volts and so set the grid voltages, whilst the main H.T. battery provided the necessary 120 volts for the valves and amplification.

The bias battery had from four to six wires plugged into it to select different voltages, and since there was universal ignorance of anything electrical at that time, no one had any idea which voltage each wire had to be plugged into. Consequently every valve was over or under biased which resulted in distortion. Mostly it went unnoticed however, as whistles, crackles, and loss of volume, were the accepted standard of radio reception for most of the time.

I was *for ever* messing about with electrical bits and pieces even at that young age, and if I could get hold of a copy of 'Practical Wireless' I would devour it word for word. I built my first wireless set before the war, albeit only a crystal set, but it was a start. My first valve set followed soon afterwards, made from instructions in my bible the 'Practical Wireless'. The early wireless sets were a simple circuit and used only three or four valves.

Much later the superhet circuit (or super-heterodyne to be exact), was introduced and this utilised dual-purpose valves and more powerful push-pull audio amplifiers. But these were powered *off the mains* by then.

At the age of eleven, all school children were required to take an examination that was called 'The Eleven Plus.' That much-feared milestone decided whether you were sent to a Grammar School, or a standard Secondary School. I failed dismally and so I was relegated to a low attainment Secondary School.

So I left junior school and we moved from the rooms we rented above the shop, I was genuinely sorry to leave that place as the shop held a fascination for me and in some strange way I felt that I belonged there. Perhaps that was because it was our first real home as a family, with the freedom to be ourselves away from Grandma.

I can still visualise the shop with its rows of wooden drawers with their various contents declared in gold letters, baskets and buckets hung from the ceiling, a forest of sacks along one wall, and overall the indefinable smell of tea, cheese, soap, oats, disinfectant, fresh ground coffee and paraffin, all mixed together.

The well-worn wooden floorboards creaked as you walked across them, and when I swept the shop floor I had to scatter wet sawdust down first in order to trap the dust. After sweeping, little lines of clean sawdust could be seen as it became trapped in rows between the boards. Mice were a problem with all the various corn products, and the cheese crumbs, and scraps from the bacon slicer. A wiry old tabby cat was locked in the shop every night to earn his keep, but all the sacks had to be folded shut first and a bundle of firewood was placed on top of each sack to stop the cat from sleeping on it.

Any public health inspector of today would have had a fit at the level of hygiene employed in those days, but I cannot recall that we ever suffered from food poisoning. Eating one *peck of dirt* generated antibodies that took care of the next *peck*, and so our bodies coped adequately with the prevailing conditions. Personally I think that extreme clinical hygiene can be detrimental to the body's ability to cope with infection. As a child I had every childhood ailment and infection that was going. At one time or another I caught, Measles, Mumps, Chicken pox, Tonsillitis, Whooping cough, Scarlet fever and

Diphtheria, but I survived them all and I am completely convinced that my immune system is now much better for it.

But back to that dusty old shop - I am glad to say that it never did catch fire or blow up, and I am pleased to be able to record what it was like when I knew it. That old shop at No.180 has been **modernised** now, it is now 'tongue and grove' boarded inside and painted white. The upstairs flat has its own front door, and the shop is narrower by the width of a passageway. All trace of the old character has gone.

As I peered in through the whitewashed glass recently, I could recall it like a scene from Dickens' Great Expectations, and I could have sworn that I saw the ghost of Mr.Galmondsway standing behind his counter smiling at me as if to say - 'It is progress lad, times change, never mind'.

The paper shop next door is still in business but he doesn't sell 'Penny plain' and 'Tuppence coloured', and he hasn't got The Boy's Own Paper either, but he has got 'Playboy' on the top shelf.

You are right, Mr.Galmondsway, time changes things.

No longer do horses puff and pant to get up Higham Hill. We lads no longer risk life and limb by careering downhill in pram-wheel carts made of soapboxes without brakes, with six marbles for the first one to reach Oats' chip shop at the bottom.

We thought we were real villains if we knocked on someone's door and then ran away to hide and watch them look for the caller. We called it *Knocking down Ginger.* Today's villains would smash your window, and then bash you on the head when you rush out to catch them. If you ran fast enough and managed to catch one, applying the time honoured *clip round the ear,* would result in *you* facing the long arm of the law today.

Yes – Time changes people and attitudes, and sadly not always for the better. There are some aspects of those times that I have been sorry to see devalued by a minority of today's younger generation.

Values like consideration for others and respect for their property, a healthy regard for the law and the consequences of breaking it, and an intuitive sense of what is right and acceptable, and of what isn't. -

But then my elders probably said the same thing about me.

At this point I am asking myself. - *What consequences of breaking it?* But I had better not go down that road, it leads to madness.

1935 - 1939

As I said we moved. Removal vans cost money and that was as scarce as ever, the distance was nearly a mile and Dad moved all the furniture a bit at a time with a borrowed totters handcart.

Dad pulled, I pushed and Mum carried odds and ends in bags, and the cat rode on the cart. I can recall that two men - strangers - helped us to push the load up the far side of Higham Hill without being asked.

We didn't have much, two beds and a few sticks of furniture, but it took several journeys to move it all. After the first trip we left mum and the bags at the new house while dad and I went backwards and forwards ferrying the rest of our meagre goods and chattels. It was all the bits and bobs that took up such a lot of space on the barrow.

I remember struggling with the beds. The top and bottom were made of solid cast-iron, with a brass knob on each corner, and the base frame consisted of two lengths of hard wood secured into two cast-iron bars that slotted into the ends. This frame supported an interwoven curly wire spring that sagged in the middle like a hammock after a few years use. Ours had seen many a year's use even before we got it, so dad bound yards of upholstery webbing tightly across the frame to improve things.

My single bed was in a better condition as it was only second hand from Auntie Daisy.

A spinster lady owned the terraced house that was to be our new home. She retreated into the two upstairs back rooms, and we rented the rest of the house. We had the front room, middle room (mine), kitchen and scullery. Upstairs we had the front bedroom, and a box-room. The sad bathroom we shared with the old lady, but at least we had a bath with a tap and a plug. Cold water or not, it was a big advance on the old tin bath. Carrying the hot water upstairs in a bucket was a small price to pay for such luxury.

Our new home, being in a terrace, was long from front to back, and narrow. Entering the front door for the first time I stood at one end of a passageway, to my left was the door to the front room, and ahead was a staircase. The passage turned left and right to continue alongside the staircase. On the immediate left of the bend, a door stood open to what was to be my very own room. At the end of the passage another door and a step down, led into the living room with a kitchen beyond that. The door to the garden led off the kitchen.

The front room had the benefit of a small bay window, and all the windows to the remainder of the house were in the sidewall facing the corresponding windows of the house next door, about three metres away. Lace curtains were very popular.

That place set us back ten bob a week (ten shillings - about one day's wages). The house was at the bottom end of Somers Road, close to Palmerstone Road, in Walthamstow.

A year or two later we reached the heights of real luxury when dad and our landlady shared the cost of installing an Ascot gas water heater in the bathroom at the top of the stairs.

Just think - running hot water - how fantastic ! But it was a different story out in the loo.

The toilet with its fixed wooden seat could only be entered from outside in the garden, round at the back of the house. When it rained - you ran. But when it was icy - you went slowly however urgent your need. You were probably carrying a bucket of water because the cistern was frozen again, together with a paraffin lamp if it was dark. The wind whistling through the ill-fitting door always blew the candle out in wintertime, so we used a storm lantern. An old piece of carpet on the floor was a big asset, because it could be propped up against the bottom of the door on the inside to keep the draught out. If we could afford the paraffin, we sometimes left the storm lantern hanging beneath the cistern so that its feeble heat would keep the water from freezing.

Newspaper, tissue paper, or any other suitable paper was cut into squares and tied with a piece of string through one corner. This hung on a nail behind the door of the loo, but it wasn't very effective and unpleasant to use. Mum would buy a roll of Jeyes whenever she could afford it, but even that was hard and shiny. Soft loo paper in rolls was not affordable until much later.

Speaking of carpet, all the floors in our house were covered in linoleum, or lino as we called it. Linoleum - made from powdered cork on a canvas backing, was the forerunner of the modern vinyl floor covering.

Needless to say we didn't have wall to wall carpet, just a few rugs scattered on the cold lino was the nearest that we came to carpets.

The lino floors were scrubbed regularly, family rooms once a week, bedrooms once a month and the front doorstep almost daily. The neighbours judged your standard by the whiteness of your front door step, so it was important to keep that clean.

Across from our house there was an alleyway that gave access to the open-air East End market, known as Walthamstow High Street. That market was open six days a week, and it became my playground.

The High Street is over a mile long and it stretches from Hoe Street Station at the top, down to St.James Street Station at the bottom. These stations are on the Chingford to Liverpool Street line. Steam trains of course. Hoe Street Station is now called Walthamstow Central, and it is now also a terminus for the Victoria Line on London's underground system.

The market was lined on both sides with cheek by jowl shops, with the pavement edge along each side occupied by stalls. Never a space unless the stallholder was ill, or otherwise unavoidably detained. Possibly even at Her Majesty's pleasure. Market stalls today are easily dismantled and packed into a van at the end of the day's trading, but in 1935 they were more permanently constructed and fitted with wheels.

At the end of the day they were trundled away to be stored in sheds and yards conveniently situated off the adjacent back streets, so leaving the High Street clear for the army of Council dustmen and sweepers. The stallholders paid rent to the Council, who in turn paid for the market to be cleaned, and they did a marvellously speedy job

Closing time in the market, when stallholders were packing up their wares, was the time when Lilly made her appearance. She was a wizened old lady whose stooped old body was clothed in a coat with huge pockets, over something woollen but indefinable. Her long grey skirt reached down to an equally old pair of lace-up boots. Her hair hung down, like Ivy from a hanging basket, and a careworn face with twinkling eyes peered out from beneath a large brimmed felt hat. She was one of the market characters, everyone knew Old Lil. As the stalls were wheeled away, there she would be, sorting through the remains with her old walking stick, retrieving anything edible or usable.

A truly inscrutable character, she could have been either destitute or a wealthy eccentric miser, for all that anyone ever knew of her.

But she and her cronies always found enough food to fill their bags, and more besides, they were the magpies of the market. I know for a fact that many traders purposely left half a box of good stuff on top of the rubbish pile for these poor devils to find, especially on a Saturday if they had had a good week.

One Thursday Mum found sixpence in the street and I saw tears in her eyes. I couldn't understand why she was crying, I thought that she would be happy. I didn't realise then that she was flat broke and waiting for the housekeeping money on Friday. That sixpence was the difference between a meal that night and nothing at all. The amazing thing was that she could conjure up a family meal for a sixpence.

One time when Mum was *on her uppers* (a reference to shoes being so badly worn that they were onto the uppers.), the kitchen chimney caught alight. Thick black smoke started belching from the chimney and sparks soon followed. We had to put the fire out and quickly. The accepted way of doing this was to empty a shovel-full of salt onto the fire.

Salt put a fire out, sugar made it burn. So Mum sent me with a penny to fetch a block of cooking salt urgently from a shop in the market. It was, I remember, a bright new penny and I ran with it through the alleyway that connected our road directly to the High St. market. Plonking the penny on the counter I said ;

'Block of salt please'. Quickly I tucked the large salt block under my arm and made to leave. The assistant called out

'Hang on a minute sonny, don't forget your change' and she gave me two shillings and five pence.

I grabbed it and ran, and I didn't stop running until I got inside our front door. Mum grabbed the salt and dealt swiftly with the fire. We couldn't relight it until the sweep had been, and that was another five bob to find. When Mum stopped to think about the change, she said the girl had mistaken the new penny for a half-crown, and that she would take the change back in the morning. But I think the family's needs overcame her honesty and I am sure she kept the cash, especially as it was halfway to paying for the sweep. I got a penny for sweets – that's how I know.

I had to earn my own pocket money or go without, so I helped on the market stalls most Saturdays and after school, fetching and carrying and getting tea in cans from the nearest café, or caff as we called it. I fetched tea in a white enamelled one-pint can with a wire handle, and the detachable lid was shaped to serve as a cup. A billy of tea and a bacon sarn'y was the usual morning order. A toasted tea cake was usually the afternoon choice.

I spoke broad Cockney then and I knew most of the rhyming slang. Contrary to common belief it wasn't used all the time, because a diatribe in complete rhyming slang would be totally incomprehensible. Rhyming slang always used two words to describe one, and the second of the two words rhymed with the word it replaced. For instance; 'Boat race' rhymes with 'face'. So your Face becomes your Boat. Simple it is not !
Dicky Dirt - Shirt, Daisy roots - Boots, Barnet Fair - Hair - and so on.

So a Cockney would put on his *dicky*, clean his *daisies* and comb his *barnet*. Since the last word is often omitted there is no clue to what the slang word means, unless you learn it at a cockney's knee, *so to speak.*

Here is an example; I went up the apples t' change me roundme's an' put on me whistle n' a titfer. Then I went fer a ball darn the frog t' the rubber dub, fur a gay an' frisky. Cos I'd 'ad a bull n' cow wiv me ol' china over 'is cock sparrer.

Translation; I went up the **apples and pears** (stairs) to change my **round-the-houses** (trousers) and to put on my **whistle and flute** (suit) and a **tit for tat** (hat). Then I went for a **ball of chalk** (walk) down the **frog and toad** (road) to the **rubber dub** (pub) for a **gay and frisky** (whisky) because I had had a **bull and cow** (row) with my old **china plate** (mate) over his **cock sparrow** (barrow). ... Would you Adam and Eve it ? (believe it?)

It is made even more complicated by the fact that there can be several rhyming slangs for the same word. For instance there are at least six for the word 'head', from Uncle Ned to Brown Bread.

What our friend was more likely to have said was; 'I went up t' change me togs n'den went darn t' the pub fir a snifta, corse I'd 'ad a ding dong wiv me mate abart 'is barra.'

My own diction gradually improved and I began to shed the Cockney from around the age of twenty at the end of the war, but the East London vowels remain.

I mention this here in some detail because the old close-knit self-supporting Cockney Community, is fast disappearing. The Blitz started it by literally breaking up the old order, then the advent of high rise flats separated families from each other and destroyed the camaraderie, and finally ethnic infiltration is finishing the job. The East End dialect is still in evidence but the use of Cockney slang is the exception now rather than the rule.

I wandered down The High Street recently and I was surrounded on all sides by voices speaking foreign tongues; African, Pakistani, Chinese, and many others that I couldn't identify. Stallholders of many varied nationalities shouted their wares, and I found it jarred slightly on my remembered images, when I heard people of ethnic origins speaking with a cockney dialect. There were turbans, and dreadlocks, and yashmaks, I even saw a fez. The cultural change was, I suppose, inevitable and probably no bad thing, but I must admit that I found it sad, like the death of a very dear friend.

The old cockney markets of Petticoat Lane and Brick Lane in Shoreditch still function, but now they are mainly a Bangladeshi area.

Any road up (any-way) - back to the High Street as it was, - I used to take home empty wooden orange and apple boxes from the market, which I would saw up and chop into sticks for fire lighting. I used to tie these into bundles and sell them on Sunday morning before Sunday School. I got a penny a bundle for them and there was always a good demand as fires were used for cooking as much as gas cookers. Egg crates were in use in those days, they were five feet long by two feet wide and about eight inches deep and made of rough wood slats. Each crate held twelve dozen eggs in two layers, packed in straw. They were good for firewood but I suffered from the splinters and preferred soapboxes, or orange boxes. I saved and straightened the nails too, and sold or exchanged them.

Saturday mornings meant the kid's matinee *up the pictures*. This was always a mad rush as we got over an hours film show for *two copper coins*, and we always left with the hero in an impossible position of certain death - which he got out of quite simply the following week. Sometimes we went to the Carlton Cinema in the High Street on the corner of Buxton Road, but that was a bit of a flea pit at that time and I preferred the Granada in Hoe Street. We saw Cowboys and Indians, Tom Mix, Laurel and Hardy, Rin Tin Tin, and of course the mandatory cartoons.

When the villain crept up on the hero, we all shouted 'Look behind you', or 'Look out he's got a gun', or similar advice which always went unheeded although we shouted loud enough.

'Is 'e deaf or summink?' we wondered.

Sometimes, or should I say often, the film broke leaving a blank screen. Then the uproar of shouts and whistling was deafening until the projectionist managed to get the film rewound, and even then when the film restarted, the cheers went on for some time. If we could, we went up into the circle, and then we threw things down onto the kids below, usually stuff we had picked up from the market on the way in.

My favourite weapon was a peashooter - a tin tube used as a blowpipe to fire dried peas. With practice they could be very accurate up to a range of twenty feet or more.

On Saturdays the market stayed open until ten or eleven o'clock at night, I loved it then. The stalls were lit by paraffin pressure lamps. These lamps had to be pumped up every so often, and I can still recall the hiss of them as a background to the cries of the traders. There was an indefinable atmosphere of noise and smells, which I can remember but not adequately describe. The feeble electric light from the shops blended with the glare from the pressure lamps on the stalls, throwing patches of light onto shoppers clutching their bags of goodies, trying to squeeze past those that had stopped to listen to a grafter spieling his wares. Little children at knee height, who had got lost in a forest of legs and bottoms, called for mum. The hubbub of voices and the cries of the traders, mingled with the smell of flowers, fish, vegetables, or fried onions and saveloys, depending on which stall you happened to be passing.

On the next corner the aroma of roasted chestnuts or baked potatoes would assail your nostrils. Whether it was a warm balmy summer evening, or a cold snowy night, the atmosphere was always the same, warm friendly and companionable. I can best describe it as a Christmas feeling of all round goodwill. At least that is how it seemed to me.

Butchers shops put a table outside about nine o'clock in the evening when the rush had died down. In my mind's eye I can see now, a rotund butcher in his blue and white striped apron, with a straw boater on his head, selling hot saveloys and pease pudding. While another butcher a few doors further along, would specialise in freshly made faggots and mashed potatoes served in greaseproof bags.

Last thing on a Saturday night it was possible to buy a joint of meat for Sunday for two bob (two shillings) or a half crown, because butchers didn't have refrigerators then, and if we ever had a Sunday joint, that is when it was bought.

People wandered about in the eerie light from the lamps, eating things out of paper clutched in their hands. People jostled together stopping to look or stopping to talk, and the kids played touch in and out of the stalls. Last minute bargains were haggled over and a nice fat chicken for the pot became half price or less at *the last knocking*, (a Cockney reference to an auction). Chestnuts were too expensive for my pocket money, but you could buy a hot baked spud from the Hot Potato Man. Penny for a large one, or an 'apenny not so large, salt free but don't waste it. How we enjoyed scrunching into the hard skin and burning our lips on the soft salty potato filling, while the heat diffused through the newspaper to warm our cold fingers. Bliss, for a penny or less.

Manzies the pie and eel shop were always busy selling Pie and Mash with parsley sauce, for a tanner (sixpence) or jellied eels in a waxed carton for the same price. Sometimes we went in, to squeeze into the wooden benches either side of the scrubbed tables, to devour our steak pie and mash with liquor of course. Outside on the stall, large metal trays of eels awaited their fate. Beside the stall stood the eel man, with his sleeves rolled up and his apron covered with the blood of slaughtered eels. Eels wriggled in the trays, wriggled in the pan of the scales, and still they wriggled even with their heads deftly cut off, until they were reduced to mouth sized pieces, to be cooked at home.

If you couldn't wait until later, cooked eels in jelly were available in the shop, or hot stewed eels, with or without mashed potato. Customers could have a spoon and a fork to eat with, provided they sat down at one of the tables. Manzies Eel and Pie shops were as familiar, and as popular, as fish and chips in those pre-war days. Outside in the street, kids would stare mesmerised by the wriggling eels.

Occasionally a hungry child might *nick* the odd piece of fruit off a stall sometimes, but I never did hear of any pickpockets, and certainly never a mugging. The costers would have killed him.

One time I was in the market when I saw a coin on the pavement and I bent down to pick it up. As I did so I saw in front of my face a pair of unusual slippers and baggy linen trousers tied round the ankles above them. I stood up to find a walnut looking face within inches of mine, and it was scowling. A gruff authoritative voice came though an unruly beard and it said;

'That belongs to God'. To me it sounded like God himself.

At the same time a gnarled brown hand with a pale palm was stuck under my nose. The authority was compelling and not to be denied, so in a kind of mesmerised daze, I put the coin into the outstretched palm. With the speed of a trap, the hand closed, its owner turned and walked away and soon became merged into the crowd. The whole thing had taken less then a minute and I was left standing there dumbstruck. That interlude became engraved into my memory when I realised that I had been conned, tricked out of a half-crown which was as much mine as Gods, and what would God want it for anyway?

Above the cries of the stallholders - 'ere you go, loverly tomartas, tanner the lot, oo wants 'em?' could just be heard the guttural lament of 'I gotta horse I 'av, - I gotta horse' and from that direction some feathers could just be seen bobbing along above the heads of the crowd.

Slowly a familiar oddball came into view, dressed in flowing robes of many colours with a full Indian head-dress. He looked very imposing, but whether the dark skin was authentic or not, I never knew, but I don't recall seeing him out in the rain. He would sell you a fully guaranteed racing certainty - 'Can't lose Guv.' - for a paltry sixpence. Each of his magical forecasts were contained in a small coloured envelope, which his trained parrot would select especially for you from a tray. Very clever because if you were to lose your bet - which you most probably would - he could always blame the parrot! I expect the mess on the back shoulder of his robes could be blamed on the parrot too.

In the market at that time many varied characters were to be seen wandering up and down the street, each with his own way of relieving shoppers of a few coins. They were always on the move because in that way they didn't have to pay for the hire of a pitch, and as long as they didn't commit a nuisance, or push a barrow, they were tolerated. They added a bit of colour and character to the market anyway.

Often to be seen in the market, was a leg-less veteran of the first world war who transported himself about in an ancient wheelchair. Under a formidable array of medals, he had a tray fitted to the front of the chair, from which he sold bootlaces and matches. More often than not coins clinked into his tin without any of his precious stock being sacrificed. When stallholders gave him the odd gift from their stall, his ever-smiling nut brown face would break into a grin showing a line of brown teeth between grey whiskers. He had an old cycle cape and sou'wester hat that he donned when it rained.

Before refrigerators, butchers shops and fishmongers had to rely on insulated cupboards partly filled with huge ice blocks to keep their stock fresh. These blocks were about one foot square by two feet long. (300 x 300 x 600mm.) The iceman delivered these on a flatbed cart pulled by a single horse. He delivered to the fish stalls in the market too, and he handled the blocks with vicious looking hooks and a huge pair of spiked tongs. He was always in a mad rush, and would dash about with his sack barrow leaving a trail of water, as he shouted *'Mind yer backs there'*.

He delivered boxes of crushed ice too, but these were used mainly by the fishmongers. In the hot weather the ice soon melted and so the iceman was always in a frenzied rush to keep up with demand and to deliver before his stock melted to nothing.

If any one thing epitomises life in those days for me, it is the barrel organ. I always thought of them as half a piano on wheels, with shafts. The sound of those nostalgic machines and the songs that they played, still sends a thrill through my memory of hard but happy times. The buskers were usually men on the dole who could rustle up a shilling to hire the organ for a day, and chance making a profit from people as hard up as they were.

The hire of an organ varied in price from a shilling to half-a-crown (two shillings and sixpence) a day, and that depended upon the number of tunes that it could play. The bigger ones were only viable outside a picture house or the variety theatre on a Friday or a Saturday evening.

One old man that I can remember seeing more than once wore a battered old top hat and a silk scarf. The scarf concealed the fact that he probably wore no collar to his tatty shirt and it drew attention away from the old boots which paddled in the water along the gutter.

The theatre queues appreciated the gesture and he collected many coins in an equally battered policeman's helmet that hung on the front of the organ for that purpose.

I used to stand around outside the Walthamstow Palace Variety Theatre for the simple pleasure of listening to the barrel organs.

Sometimes in my early 'teens, I took a girlfriend to the pictures. In those days the back row of the stalls and the circle, had the arm-rest removed from every other seat and that made it a lot easier to have a cuddle. Snogging seats, we called them. I remember one time that my girl was wearing a fur coat (imitation, no doubt) and we shared a small bar of Cadbury's chocolate. The bar was on my knee when she folded her legs across my lap. I forgot about the chocolate from that point on, but I remember that we left the cinema with a melted brown mess all down the front of my trousers and all over the back of her coat.

A picture house programme then, consisted of the main picture, with a supporting 'B grade' repeat, and the Pathē Newsreel. These three would be run continuously and the audience simply walked in at any time, so that if you missed the start of a picture you simply waited for it to come round again. Then to the observation *This is where we came in* - you stood up and left. There was always the option of staying put and seeing the whole film again. We teenagers never watched the film anyway, and the back seat was just somewhere convenient and warm to have a good snog in the dark.

Home entertainment relied on the wireless. We didn't play the piano or sing songs, some families did, but we didn't. Just as well really because no-one could sing in tune. The old *Joe Anna* did a turn at parties though, and after a few pints, staying in tune didn't seem to matter.

Apart from the wireless, we did have an old wind-up gramophone at home, that Dad had managed to scrounge from somewhere. The sound box on the end of the arm weighed a ton, I dropped it once and the steel needle nailed Dad's record of The Messiah to the turntable. He never did forgive me for that. Later we got some fibre needles that we had to sharpen every time. Instead of the horn being on the top of the gramophone, it was inside the wooden body on ours, and the loudness could be adjusted by opening or closing the doors at the front,- very technical !

With the top horn type of gramophone, as in the H.M.V trade mark, it was usual to quieten the sound by stuffing something woollen down inside the horn. From that practice came the expression *put a sock in it* meaning *be quiet or shut up*.

The gramophone records were ten or twelve inches in diameter and made of a black plastic material, and seventy-eight r.p.m. was the only speed, but we thought it was wonderful.

It was certainly a big improvement on Auntie Olive playing on our bashed about piano with its brass candlesticks and three black keys that didn't work.

The early gramophone records were made of a hard bakelite material but later ones were produced from a softer plastic derived from milk residue. The same material was used to make buttons in those days before modern plastics. When we could get any old records we used to heat them up in front of the fire until they became soft and then we moulded them over an upturned bowl into dishes with wavy edges. Sometimes we painted these and sold them for a copper or two.

We had a cat - a scruffy old tabby, necessary in those days to keep the mice in check. Cat food wasn't in tins from the supermarket. - What's a supermarket? - We could hardly afford food for ourselves let alone the cat. But he was allocated sixpence a week for his keep as long as Mum saw no mice. The 'Cats meat man' delivered cat's meat every day, it was cooked horseflesh sliced and skewered on a wooden stick. He would push this meal through the letterbox to the moggy waiting behind the door, and he knocked every Saturday for his sixpence. The cat always knew when he was coming, and even I could smell him from several doors away if the wind was in that direction. Goodness knows how 'Mrs.Cats meat man' put up with him, but at least he earned a living of sorts I suppose, and it was honest work. Certainly the cat was grateful. He had scraps on Sunday for a change.

One of the popular traders that plied the streets scratching a living, was the Walls' ice-cream man who pedalled his 'Stop Me and Buy One'. (perhaps a description is necessary here for any younger readers). Imagine a box about 50.Cm wide, by 60.Cm long and 50.Cm deep. Fix a bicycle wheel on opposing sides, and a handlebar on one end. Now take the back half of a sturdy bicycle - Wheel, pedals and saddle - and attach this to the underside of the box so that the box can twist from side to side. You now have a tricycle with a box between the two front wheels. To steer the contraption it was necessary to swing the whole box from side to side. A metal box with a lid was fitted inside the outer box and the space between was filled with dry ice. All that remains is to paint it dark blue and write on the front STOP ME AND BUY ONE in white letters. There you have it - A Walls' ice cream cart.

A credit card sized lump of ice cream, 25mm thick, wrapped in paper cost one penny, vanilla or chocolate. And water ice, lemon or orange flavoured, in a triangular cardboard tube cost a 'appeny. I used to buy a 'appeny half of a choc ice, cut from corner to corner by the ice-cream man, under the watchful eye of the purchaser - me - to ensure I didn't get short measure. I could seldom afford to buy a whole one but when I did - Heaven ! I am still very fond of ice cream to this day, and I eat more of it than I should.

Speaking of box-tricycles brings to mind another character who also used one, and that was a white haired and bearded old chap we called Andy. He had a converted ice cream tricycle with the insides taken out, and the outside painted a bright yellow. He would pedal the streets in all weathers calling *"Always 'andy - they are - they are - they're always 'andy.'* He sold buttons, needles, safety pins, darning wool, cottons, ribbons, and general haberdashery, all stuffed into his tricycle or hanging from the sides. He had a huge black umbrella with a broken handle that he tied over the box when it rained. This yellow box with a black dome on top could often be seen parked outside the local cafē when the weather was bad.

Poor old Andy had a hard time of it when it rained as did all the other totters and costermongers who earned their living outdoors. Not for them nice cosy warm vans from which to trade.

Another street pedlar (a small trader, not a rider of bicycles !) also had a bicycle contraption. He had fixed a grindstone to the crossbar of his bike and attached this by a second chain to the pedals. He would prop the back wheel on a stand, pedal like mad and sharpen anything made of steel, from knives to scissors and hedging shears, for a very modest copper or two. *'Anyfink t' sharpen'* was his cry. What a happy character he was. He had a podgy round face and body to match, but he was always laughing and joking. Quite a little ray of sunshine, everybody liked him. He would sharpen a kids penknife for free, but only if you said 'Please'.

So many people worked outdoors in the streets. When employment was scarce, men with families to support became self employed doing anything that would earn a little money. Window cleaning, gardening, hedge cutting, and even collecting and selling horse manure. At least it was honest work and it eked out the dole money. It must have been heartbreaking for grown family men trying to *raise the rent* in such circumstances.

I was totally un-aware of the deprivation. Partly because I was only young, and partly because, quite simply, that is the way things were.

Gladys - I have just remembered Gladys, or old Gladrags as we knew her, she was a flower lady, and could be seen in the latter part of the week sitting behind her huge wickerwork basket on an apple box. Her pitch was always outside the railway station on a Friday evening, otherwise on the corner of Palmerstone Road halfway up the market.

Her voluminous felt skirt spread across her thighs and hung down to the ground, under there and inside her apple box seat, she kept her sandwiches and her money safe from all but a hurricane. That snug little space was also home to her little terrier dog. He - or she- was a scruffy little mongrel, black with a single white patch over one eye. It was obvious that they doted on each other, and I never saw them apart.

You may well be wondering how I knew what went on under her skirt. – Well, I happened to be there one day when a curious little kitten decided to crawl under there to find out for itself. She found the dog, and the resulting fracas caused Glad to leap up, revealing all. – well, almost all. Were it not for the kitten you would never have known either. On the worktop of her lap, when it wasn't occupied by the dog, she bound up bunches of flowers and wrapped posies of forget-me-nots with her deft, mitten clad fingers. Her rotund face would peer over her wickerwork basket, with those huge horn-rimmed glasses making her look like an inquisitive owl in a woollen hat. She called everyone 'Dearie' in a kind of gravelly voice that you would expect to hear from a man. *'Loverly daffs, only a tanner dearie, gorn y' cn afford 'at can't yer? git 'em fer y'missis'.* She only sat in the market at weekends because that was the only time when folks were likely to have money to spare for flowers. On Sunday mornings she would take up her usual pitch outside the cemetery.

The chimney sweep was yet another trader who earned his living on the streets. He pushed a handcart, with bags for the soot, and a set of rods and brushes. Every time that I saw the sweep he made me laugh, for his black soot grimed face reminded me of an old time nigger-minstrel or one of the golliwogs from a jar of Robinson's jam. Housewives couldn't telephone for a sweep then. If you were in need of one you had to keep an eye open for him on his rounds, or put the word out

'If yer see Sweepy, tell him to knock at number five will yer ducks?

He charged five bob if you let him keep the soot. I wonder what he did with it?

The coal-man came on Saturdays with his flat bed cart. It had no sides, just a low fence at the front with a driver's seat perched above it. Sacks of coal leaned against this fence and then other sacks against them, and so on towards the back of the cart. At the very back sat a neat pile of emptied sacks carefully folded. A full sack would be dragged towards the edge of the cart, and then the coal-man expertly tucked his shoulder under it and carried it, with one hand on the open edge, to steady the load.

He wore a hood made from a fairly new and clean sack to keep the coal from going down his neck. The hood was fashioned by tucking one bottom corner of the sack back inside itself until it was folded down the centre and the two corners were together. This formed a double thickness half sack which he wore over his head and down his back. All the coal-men I ever knew wore this hood, as well as a generous layer of coal dust, like a badge of office.

Our order of one bag of 'small nuts' would by tipped down the 'coal hole' by the front door where if fell into the cellar below. Coal was cheaper by the half ton, but we seldom had enough money for more than one bag at a time. We used the coal to start the fire, and then we burned the less expensive coke or Coalite. Coal dust was spread on an old newspaper, which would then be tightly rolled and twisted until the ends could be tucked in to form a bun. We burned these 'bricks' sometimes when we were out of fuel. If there was a lot of dust and small crumbs of coal left, Dad would mix these with water to bind them and then fill small cardboard boxes with the mixture and leave them to dry. These 'coal bricks' burned well and saved a lot of waste.

Down at the bottom of the high street, Trams used to run along Blackhorse Road, and past St James street station. In between the tramlines the roads were surfaced with blocks of wood wedged in to keep the lines in place and to make a quieter ride. These blocks became soaked in road tar and when repairs were made, and broken ones replaced, Dad would bring some home from the council yard in a sack dangling from the handlebars of his bike. He got them 'for nuffink' and they *burned a treat*, but they *didn't half soot up the chimney*. Mounted beneath the tram was a huge bell, and the clanger was operated by a steel mushroom that stuck up through the floor of the drivers cab. One stamp on the mushroom equalled one clang of the bell. The tram speed was regulated by means of a rotating lever with a brass knob on the end. As the lever rotated it activated a ratchet like catch that made a very loud clicking noise.

Anyone whoever travelled on one of those old trams will always remember the sound - Clang, clang, click-click, click-click-click, and ear rending screeches as the wheels grated on the curve of the rails round the tight corner by Woolworths at the bottom of the High Street. The front of a tram was the same as the back, because they didn't turn round at the terminus. The driver simply walked to the other end, plugged in his lever and off he went in reverse. When we kids got on at the back we always stamped on the bell mushroom at least once, before we ran up the stairs to the open air top deck. Trams with a closed in top came later.

Dad progressed in his job and became a supervisor in the Cleansing Department of the local Borough Council, but even so his wages still remained poor. So did we, with a growing family, because Mum was pregnant again and an addition to our family was due at any moment.

I wasn't at all sure what was going on at the time, as it was all kept under wraps, but I found out later.

Mum went away and came back with my brand new baby sister. Dad was delighted but I can't remember being very excited myself by the turn of events, and I suspect that apart from a natural curiosity, I was not very interested. Perhaps it was because mum had less time for me.

I do remember the baby spent a lot of time being bathed in the kitchen sink, and I wondered why her little bum went right round to the front, but I didn't like to say anything. Well you don't do you, when you are young. Sometimes you blurt things straight out, and sometimes you are far too embarrassed to let your ignorance show, especially on that subject so I kept quiet. I thought 'If there is something wrong with her perhaps they will tell me later', but they never did mention it.

My education in that department was sadly lacking. At the age of thirteen I knew nothing about the reproductive process, and without elder brothers or sisters there wasn't anyone to tell me, and the subject was never spoken of at school. Not to me anyway.

Across the road, further up, a girl of about eighteen went away for a week. When she came back her mum had a new baby boy, and she had a new brother. Or so I was told, but the neighbours knew the truth I expect, because there were a lot of whispers about it at the time.

Mother, meantime, had her hands full with the housework and a new baby to care for, and I noticed that I was given a lot more chores to do while being bribed with the title of 'Man of the house'. I was told what a grownup thing it was to be left in charge of my baby sister. I fell for that, and in consequence I did a lot of babysitting. Apart from that though, nothing changed as far as I was concerned.

I used to enjoy watching the road gangs on my way home from school. There were no pneumatic drills in those days, and roads were broken up with hammer and chisel. The gangs worked in teams of four or five, usually five. One man held the massive chisel in a pair of tongs about four feet long, whilst the others spaced them-selves round in a circle, each with a long handled fourteen pound hammer. They would then strike the chisel one after the other in a continuous rhythm; 1-2-3-4-1-2-3-4-1-2-3-4 and so on like the pistons of an engine.

They dressed in a shirt without a collar, worn over long sleeved vests, corduroy trousers, belt and braces, string tied round the trouser legs just below the knee, heavy boots with reinforced toe caps and the whole thing topped off with the inevitable cloth cap. What wonderful solid characters they were. It was a joy to watch their skill and I never tired of it. They never missed the chisel and the rhythm was perfect. When they became too old to swing a hammer or a pick, the lucky ones became a night watchman.

Close to the road works, the night watchman would erect his hut. This would be about six feet by eight and made of canvas supported on a frame of wood. In front of the hut a coke brazier would burn constantly, often made from an old oil drum pierced all over with a sharp pickaxe, and stood on bricks. It would be used to burn the tar from shovels and pickaxes, to toast huge chunks of bread, or to cook a navvy's dinner.

Many times I have seen eggs and sometimes bacon frying over the 'cokey' on a clean shovel. I also learned some fruity Cockney language too when an egg slid off the shovel into the fire. At night all the tools were stored at the back of the hut, and the watchman stood guard over them until morning. Red warning lanterns were placed around *the 'ole in the road* and it was his job to keep them alight with a refill of paraffin. If you were out late on a cold night, you could always be sure of a warm-up and a friendly chat with the watchman who would be pleased to have your company. Policemen too would be drawn to the brazier like moths to a flame, where they would share a *'cuppa'* with the *'old fella'* in the long hours of the night shift.

The High Street & the Palace Theatre

The old lady who owned our house died, and as sitting tenants we took over the whole house for an extra half-crown per week. Now that we had two spare rooms, Mum became a landlady and let out 'Digs' to the Pro's from the local variety theatre. It was just a few minutes walk from our home to the Walthamstow Palace in the High Street, and so the touring artists found it very convenient. Bed and Board cost them ten bob a week each, with two sharing a room, so that added considerably to our income.

For the very first time, we had money left at the end of the week, instead of the other way round. It meant a lot more work for Mum, but Dad and I did what we could to help, and with the extra cash Mum was able to send some of the laundry to a neighbour up the road, who *took in washing*. With the new baby to care for Mum had already given up the dress making anyway.

Sometimes, one of the speciality acts would give me a complimentary ticket to the front row of the stalls. From there I was often used as a stooge, a plant, called from the audience to assist in magic acts etc., after suitable instruction as to what I had to do. I got paid a modest fee and did well out of it, including the pass into the theatre to see the show. I distinctly remember a skating act that employed me to volunteer to be held by the arms and swung round and round at speed. The performer wore skates and stood on a small circular stage about six feet across. When he put me down, I was supposed to stagger about as if I was completely giddy. I didn't have to act, I <u>was</u> giddy and on the second night I nearly fell down into the orchestra pit, I must have been mad. The next evening he said,

'Do that again lad, you know, stagger to the edge of the stage, it got a good laugh'

So I did it for the rest of the week, but it cost him an extra sixpence, and I was learning another way to earn a few bob.

Eventually I became well known at 'The Palace' and was freely admitted at the stage door. As a young lad in the early days of puberty, the girls of the chorus were the main attraction for me. Most of them were only a few years older than I was and I got to know some of them very well. I had free access back stage and spent a lot of time in the chorus dressing room where I became *a part of the furniture*, that is unnoticed and accepted as belonging. The girls would undress and change their costumes completely oblivious of my presence, and after a while I too thought nothing of it. I used to run errands and help out in a lot of little ways. I tried to go there two or three times a week, and always on a Saturday if I could manage it.

At the end of the week they often gave me a few shillings if I had been particularly helpful, or a few kisses. To be honest I preferred the kisses, a kiss and a hug from such beautiful and friendly girls was a young man's ecstasy. I learned a lot about girls very quickly, and I grew up sexually in a hurry too. Needless to say, I loved it.

Because I could always get into the Palace via the stage door, I fetched and carried for the back-stage crew as well, so I was accepted and I saw all the shows

The nude tableaux were pretty risqué in those days and the law forbade them to move on stage. I used to stand in the wings and I saw them move, and a lot else besides.

Most of the famous names came to the Palace at one time or another on their circuit, and some stayed at our house. Wilson, Kepple and Betty, the Egyptian sand dancers, always stayed at our place and I can remember having to light the coal fires in their rooms. Plenty of wood and a splash of paraffin usually got the coal hot enough to burn, and if the coal was damp a sheet of newspaper held over the front of the grate became necessary to get enough draught to get it started. More often than not the paper scorched and caught fire resulting in a scramble to get it into the fire and not onto the fireside rug.

Sunday was change over day and always a rush to get the rooms cleaned and the beds changed *for the next lot in*. For me it was a good excuse to miss the Sunday morning service and Mum needed all the help she could get. How she managed to take care of the family, and up to four lodgers, with all the cleaning and cooking, I shall never know. There were no washing machines, or microwave ovens, in those days and we didn't own a vacuum cleaner.

The only domestic appliances available to help her with the workload, were just a gas stove to cook on, and later an Ascot water heater on the kitchen wall. But she coped somehow. At that age I didn't notice if she was overtired, overworked, or overwrought. Kids don't do they? They just take things for granted – I know I did.

One week we had a Chinese juggling act in and they asked Mum for some rice. Now Mum used to make a superb baked rice pudding with milk and nutmeg on the top, and she gave them that. She had no idea that they wanted simple boiled rice without liquid, as she had no experience of their requirements whatsoever. The Chinese endured her efforts until Wednesday when they gave up and cooked it for themselves. Dad and I were relieved as we were fed up with eating the rejected sloppy rice, with milk, without milk, too much water, or 'cut it with a knife' type of rice.

In spite of all the work, Mum always seemed to find time for me, and we spent hours together some evenings, painting and drawing, or making up 'penny plain' models. Plasticine was a favourite material, and mum was very good at modelling animals and funny faces. We used to try to make replicas of people we knew, and we laughed until the tears ran at some of our efforts. Grandma White was the butt of many hilarious facial variations.

The 'Old Palace Variety Theatre' was opened in 1903 and closed in 1954 It was finally demolished in 1960. It is now a row of eight shops, and it is called Palace Parade. The Walthamstow Baths that stood opposite it on the other side of the street has gone too. It is now an open pedestrian area with trees and bench seats, and what little remains of our recreation ground is still to be seen behind it.

We used to be taken to the Swimming Baths occasionally by the school, a whole class would be taken for a swimming lesson, and some kids, including me who didn't have a costume, had to swim in their underpants.
I don't know what the girls wore as we were never allowed to see. They were taken to the baths at a different time from us.

In another part of the building the Wash Baths were situated, and I went a couple of times with my dad. A row of wood partitioned compartments each housed a huge enamelled bathtub and a wooden bench, while the intervening strip of concrete floor was covered with slatted wooden duckboards. The compartments were end-on to a passageway, and the hot taps for the baths were on the outside wall in the passageway itself, only the cold tap was on the inside. On payment of a few coppers, the attendant would give you a small bar of yellow disinfectant soap and a rough old towel. He would then turn on the hot tap for the allotted amount of water, before shutting the door. If you were to let the cold tap run for too long you paid the penalty by having a lukewarm bath. Mum always sent us equipped with a change of underclothes, our own towel and a piece of decent soap in a canvas bag. On the rare occasion that we were pushed out of the bathroom by our lodgers, we made reluctant use of the public facility. Those public baths were a bit ancient, and the enamel baths were sometimes chipped, but they were always kept very clean.

It was fortunate that we lived so close to the market because with refrigerators not yet available we had to buy perishable food almost daily. In the hot weather even the milk would *go off* before teatime, if it wasn't boiled before mid-day. Meat, when we had any, and leftovers, were stored in a cupboard made of perforated zinc sheet. This was fixed to an outside wall in a shady corner where it was cooler than indoors. The perforated zinc had to have small holes so that the flies couldn't get in. There were always flies around somewhere, and food on the table had to be protected from them. We had several fine net covers that opened like an umbrella, and these were placed over a plate of food to keep them off. The milk or gravy jugs, and jam jars, were covered with small lace circles to which large beads had been sown round the edges. The rattle of those beads against the sides of the jug is one of many sound memories that I retain.

Another sound memory is that of a policeman's whistle. It was quite a distinctive sound, produced as it was by a tubular whistle, made of solid brass, and it had a slightly deeper tone than the type now used by football referees. Policemen were respected, and we kids often asked them for help or the right time. A policeman's uniform in those days had a high collar, like a dog collar, with a long row of silver buttons down the front. They wore a black leather belt, from which hung their truncheon, and attached to the front by a clip was a forward facing torch. The whistle, to summon help, was attached to the top pocket by a silver chain A neatly folded cape, carried over one shoulder, completed the outfit. If they ever caught you *playing up* a whack on the side of your head from their cape always had the desired effect of chastisement, since it was something that you didn't forget in a hurry. They were like universal fathers in uniform, icons of right and wrong. We didn't fear policemen - no reason to - but we always looked up to them in awe of their authority.

I have just realised the implications of what I just reported: A policeman had a whistle so that he could summon help from another policeman if necessary. That implies that policemen on the beat were seldom more than a whistle sound away from each other. If you fired a rocket today, it is unlikely that another policeman would see it. Times certainly have changed.

In this environment I spent my early 'teens and grew up to expect nothing for nothing, and to work for what I wanted. All the families round about us were *in the same boat* financially. No one had anything to brag about, so there was no one to envy.

Adults and children alike, happily shared what little there was. We didn't know it then, but that attitude was to help us survive the trauma of the war to come.

One year we saved hard and spent a week at Southend on holiday. We went by train from Blackhorse Road Station on the L.N.E.R. that is the London & North Eastern Railway, we always called it the Late & Never Early Railway. The other railways at that time were the L.M.S. - The London Midland and Scottish, the G.W.R. - The Great Western Railway, and the S.R. - The Southern Railway, which combined the old South Eastern and the South Western Railways. They used steam engines then of course. 'Puffing Billys' we called them.

On our journey to Southend, against advice I put my head out of the window and got soot smuts in my eye. Another lesson learned. My sister laughed. There were times when I didn't like my sister very much, but we were off on holiday, I had my own spending money, and I wasn't going to let a silly sister spoil it. Anyway she caught her finger playing with the leather strap that pulled the carriage window up and down, so we were even. Railway compartments in those days were the full width of the carriage, no corridors, and each was about five and a half, to six feet wide. Bench seats ran along each side, one side facing the direction of travel, and the other side *backs to the engine*. The space in between equalled the width of the door and was jammed with standing passengers in the rush hour. The door had a vertically sliding window that was pulled up, or lowered, by means of a wide leather strap with a row of holes that could be hooked over a peg below the window.

There was always an argument over whether the window should be up or down. Down to let the cigarette smoke out and the soot smuts in, or Up to keep the smoke in and the rain out. Half way was O.K. if you were not sitting in the corner, and getting a draught. If it was down, you could look out at the station and watch the guard blow his whistle, and wave his green flag with all the authority bestowed upon him by the possession of his L.N.E.R. watch tucked into a waistcoat pocket. As the train started off he would jump back aboard his guard's van at the tail end of the train.

The station porter stood at the engine end of the platform, in his railway waistcoat with sleeves. He would wait patiently until everyone had embarked, and as the train started top move, it was his job to shut any doors left open as the train pulled out. I can hear it now - slam – slam, slam - pause - slam slam. - long pause - and a louder final slam as the train gathered speed. The new arrivals tried to keep their balance while they swung their bags up onto the rope netting rack, and those seated tried to keep their feet from being trodden on.

We stayed in *Digs*, rented rooms in someone else's house by the sea. The word Digs is a part anagram corruption of Lodgings. These places were always clean with good food, but the beds were never the same as your own. We had meat puddings and good home cooking with **afters every day 'cos we was on 'oliday.** I recall that a local café sold my ideal snack, of meat pie with baked beans, for a tanner (sixpence). Dad bought me some most days, and then at the end of the week he said 'No'. I didn't know why and I made a fuss, which upset Dad quite a lot. Much later I realised that he said 'No', because he was broke, borasic lint, skint, spent out, but I just thought he was being mean. Kids can be very cruel in their ignorance, and in their face value assessments of situations.

I didn't fully appreciate my father then, not many kids do I suppose, as they are happily unaware of the problems of life. My parents were wonderful to me and gave me more than they cold afford. They never rowed or shouted at each other, leastwise never in my hearing, and so I had a very loving, calm, and moral upbringing. I have a lot to thank them for, sadly though I can only do that posthumously now.

Back to the seaside – I can see them now, Dad sitting in a deck chair with his bare feet stark white against the sand, trousers rolled up, and a with a knotted hankie perched on his head, reading a copy of 'Tit-bits'.

Behind dad the brightly painted bathing huts with their huge wheels, formed a gay backdrop, and just above them could be seen the giant wheel of the Kursaal funfair. Turn round, and there is Mum paddling at the waters edge with a bunch of skirt in her hand, showing her drawers, and just for once not having to worry about getting the dinner ready.

A cry of *'Ju-cy-pi-napple'* close by, as a pedlar tries to sell his chunks of pineapple from a tray. There goes the electric tram along the pier, carrying holidaymakers the mile to the pier-head, the minstrel show, Gypsy Rose Lee the fortune teller, and the 'what the butler saw' machines.

When mum came back with sand stuck to her legs, she sent me up to the Prom' for a beach tray of tea. So off I toddled, my bare feet covered in sand, up the wooden steps that led up to the prom', across the road - mind the trams - and then to the open window at the front of the cafe. For five bob deposit and a shilling for the tray you got a pot of freshly made tea, sugar and milk, cups and saucers and half a dozen biscuits. Anything broken had to be paid for, when you took the tray back.

Walking back with the loaded tray was difficult but I managed it. If Mum had got sandwiches, or a bag of chips with a plate of cockles, then tea never tasted better, then or since, even if you did get sand in with the sugar. Standing at the water's edge, throwing a ball and waiting for the waves to wash it back, sandcastles, wooden spades, such happy childhood memories. After lunch, Dad and I were larking about on the sand and he was kneeling down threatening to knock over my sand castle, so I jumped onto his back. I kicked his hip bone, as I jumped and I really hurt my toes. Dad took me to the St.John's Ambulance First Aid Post. I remember crying ;

'Its not broken is it? - is it?'

'No lad.' the man replied as he applied some methylated spirit with cotton wool, 'It's only sprained.' But he was wrong, my second toe was broken, and it still is.

Bathing huts - wooden sheds about four feet by six, with apex roofs - these were mounted on wheels, large wheels at the sea end and small wheels on the landward end. This arrangement kept them level against the slope of the beach and a wire rope was used to lower them into the water. By this means a bather could enter the hut through a door on the landward side, change into bathing drawers, and emerge down the steps straight into the water without being observed from the land. This was standard practice in Victorian times when bathing costumes covered all of the body. In the time of my youth the bathing huts, although permanently moored above high water, were still in use as changing rooms.

Gaily painted, they added a splash of colour to the beach even though their wheels were rusting away, and the winches to haul them had long ago ceased to function.

Changing on the beach was considered offensive in those days even if you already had a costume on underneath. Taking your clothes off in public was salacious and frowned upon, but children were allowed to change under a towel. So for a few coppers you could buy a bathing hut ticket that was valid for the whole day.

The shops that faced the sea, across the road from the prom', only sold a very limited selection of wares. There was rock everywhere, - made on the premises with *Southend* running right through it, - cockles mussels and whelk stalls, bucket and spade souvenir shops, and cafés, penny arcades, together with a liberal sprinkling of pubs that made up the limited choice on the sea front. They were all brightly painted though and they formed a riot of colour, a bit garish perhaps but it created the holiday mood that people wanted.

Many hawkers plodded up and down the beach trying to sell their wares from a tray. Walking on sand is hard work and it must have been extremely tiring to have to do it all day. Some sold ice cream of course, while others sold fruit, or sunshades, or newspapers and a magazine called Tit-bits.

I seem to remember that it was dark green in colour with white lettering. It was very popular at the time because it contained puzzles and short stories, and various items of interest. It was just the thing for lazy beach time reading. Sometimes Mum bought me a Tit-bit's mystery bag. This contained all kinds of children's goodies such as cardboard sunglasses, a Chinese wire puzzle, a fishing line complete with hook, various flags for the top of sandcastles, a little book of seaside information, riddles with the answers to catch dad with, and sometimes even a lollypop.

They were happy carefree days, when contentment was a dig in the sand and a paddle in the mud of Southend, with a fishing net clutched firmly in one hand and two tiny crabs in your tin bucket.

When we got back from our holiday, our neighbours next door went away for a few days over the weekend to visit relations, and Mum took charge of their budgie. It was kept in a cage in the back kitchen and allowed to fly free when the cage was cleaned. On the Saturday evening when I came home, without a thought for the budgie I ran down the narrow passageway, and opened the kitchen door. In a flash the budgie was going back the way I had come, but I had left the front door open hadn't I?

I reached the front gate in time to see it flying happily away over the rooftops. I recall the incident with clear mental pictures, but I cannot remember what mum said - just as well I expect.

Dad replaced the budgie, fortunately a standard colour, with another one. Luckily it was not a talker so I think the neighbours never knew. I hope dad got the right sex or Joey could become Joanna. You never can tell with budgies, can you?

About that time, I was taken seriously ill. I contracted Scarlet Fever and Diphtheria, both at the same time, and in those days that was often a fatal combination. I was whisked off to an isolation hospital and my bedroom was fumigated for forty-eight hours with a sulphur candle.

In hospital my bed was completely enclosed in glass, side by side with several other identical cubicles, and the only door opened to an outdoor veranda.

The nurse's office was at the far end and there was no means by which you could attract a nurse's attention except by waving, and that never worked after dark, as nurse was either reading, or studying, or having a much earned kip.

I remember lying there on my bed feeling very lonely. I was wearing a pair of stiff hospital pyjamas and a washed pale hospital gown. I was shut in a glass box, and all was silent.

The next day two other children were admitted into the cubicles on either side of me, and that provided company of a sort. We couldn't speak to each other, but we were able to hold comics up against the glass to exchange the funny bits.

One night I awoke desperate for a bottle, but try as I might, I couldn't get the nurse to notice me because she was bending over her desk, motionless. I decided to go outside as something had to be done, I got out of bed but the outside door was locked. I shouted as loud as I could, but the thick glass prevented me from being heard, as I was about four cubicles away from the nurse. Returning to bed, I tried my very best to contain the need, but I failed and wet the bed. Fortunately the bed had a rubber sheet over the mattress and I spent a miserable night trying not to lie in the puddle. The next morning my explanations went unheeded, and I got into terrible trouble for what I had done. They repeatedly insisted that I should have called the nurse. I fumed at the injustice of it, and I think that is the reason why I recall the incident so clearly.

Perhaps I should add that I didn't die from the illness, I recovered, with no after effects. - Put your hand up, the boy that shouted 'Pity'.

In 1937 we celebrated the Coronation of King George VI and Queen Elizabeth, who came to be known as The Queen Mother. School children were each given a Coronation mug, my one has since gone to the land of old crockery, or perhaps it is the cherished possession of someone who collects such things. For some reason the population of the East End went berserk, not in rage but in delight. Everyone took on a festive mood, flags and streamers and banners, festooned the streets. The Union Jack appeared everywhere, and, it seemed to me, everyone went *over the top* (OTT) with the joy of it.

We had a massive street party, with tables of all kinds arranged down the centre of the road, these were covered with fresh white sheets. Every one made cakes and jellies and pies and trifles and sandwiches, ad infinitum.

Four men carried out a piano from somewhere, and with endless pots of tea, bottles of fizz, and crates of beer, our street *let their hair down*. Everyone wore paper hats, blew up countless balloons, and danced and sang until well after dark. The whole thing bordered on hysteria and I could not understand what all the fuss was about. But I enjoyed the party.

A super girl of my own age, who lived up the road, was called Susan and she and I celebrated in our own quiet way, in her front room.

I have fond memories of Christmas time, not a specific one, but all of our Christmas's around that period because we always did the same thing. Christmas morning, Mum, Dad, my sister and I, we all set off for Auntie Daisy's. Now Auntie Daisy was Dad's sister and she was married to my Uncle Albert, who was a kind unassuming man. (I am named after him because my mum rather fancied him I think.) They had two daughters Nellie and Iris. Now Iris was the younger of the two and about eighteen months older than I was, and she was my idol, I loved her dearly. She liked me too, and we seldom missed the chance for a kiss and a cuddle on the sly. But we were old enough to understand the implications - when told - that we were first cousins and therefore could never be serious as a couple, nevertheless it was a bonus for me at the Christmas gathering. Olive, another of Dad's sisters and her family, together with Dad's third sister Edie, a spinster. We all assembled at 'Daisy's' on Christmas morning. Twelve in all, and that neatly avoided the problem of thirteen at table.

It was a real family Christmas, and how we all packed into that small council house in Billet Road, I shall never know, but we did.

When we had all gathered, the men went off down to the local pub, the ladies prepared dinner, and we youngsters compared and shared presents.

Christmas dinner lasted almost two hours and we wanted for

nothing. It was the one time in the year for which we had all saved and no expense was spared. Everyone gave a present to everyone else. I had saved sixpence a week and with twenty-five shillings I was able to buy a present for everybody and still have a little left over.

After dinner the men washed up and cleared away, whilst the ladies put their feet up and devoured a bottle of port (probably two) – 'With a splash of lemon please dear'. All except Auntie Edie of course, who was strictly T.T. She was strict and straight-laced in everything, but she had a heart as big as Epping Forest. She was devoutly religious (C of E) and she was *in service* in a large house in South Kensington in London. She was the housekeeper and ran the whole household including several servants and the cook. She took me there once when the master was away on holiday, and I had a great time. Cook made a fuss of me and stuffed me with food, the like of which I had only dreamed about.

Firmly planted in my memory is their toilet, it was hideous, at least I thought so. It was indoors, and that was a novelty, but it consisted of a large rectangular wooden seat, highly polished with the usual hole cut into it. But inside that hole – ugh, - the bowl was painted all over with revolting blue snakes that swirled and twisted around each other. It was gruesome. Set into the side of the seat, a large brass handle had to be pumped up and down until the bowl was full of water, and then a foot pedal affected the necessary emptying. What a contraption, it's no wonder that it remains in my mental archive.

Many years later when Auntie Edie was staying at our house over the weekend, she caught my fiancée and I doing what came naturally, on the front room carpet, at past one o'clock in the morning.

She said 'Goodnight darlings' she shut the door and never mentioned it to another soul. ...

But back to Christmas :
In the evening we played games and enjoyed the cosy companionship that comes from a close family at Christmas time. There was always a shortage of chairs, which Iris and I were pleased to take advantage of by sharing one. By eleven or twelve o'clock the ladies went up to share the available beds, and the men remained playing cards until the early hours of the morning. We youngsters stayed up until we fell asleep sprawled across the settee or curled up in an armchair. With Iris on my lap, my leg fell asleep long before I did.

In the morning the men cooked a big breakfast, and woke up the ladies with tea in bed. After breakfast the men retired to the still warm beds to be awoken at two o'clock in the afternoon of Boxing-day. We youngsters were left to our own devices on Boxing-day morning and we cousins had a wonderful time together. Whenever I think of those times, a deep warmth and a true Christmas spirit invades my recollection of Christmas in my youth. It was a big highlight in my life, and an event to be looked forward to with great expectations, and they were never disillusioned.

As I mentioned earlier, I had been saving sixpence every week in a Savings and Loan Club which Dad ran at the church, and by December I had twenty-five shillings to spend on presents. Most of this was spent at Woolworths in the High Street. It was down at the very bottom of the market, on the corner with Blackhorse Road, but it has gone now.

In Woolworths everything cost sixpence or less. I bought a small wood plane there, sixpence for the die-cast base and sixpence for the blade. I still have it and it is in regular use. In those days Woolworths didn't have the head high displays that are common today. Instead the huge floor area was covered with waist high counters and everything was displayed on the top of these, with glass partitions separating the various items. Cupboards underneath the counters housed boxes of the remaining stock.

Overhead cash containers on little trolleys whizzed *to and fro* along wires connecting several cash points to the cashier's box set high up at one end of the store. The eyes of the cashier's assistant were the CCTV of the day.

In my memory I can still hear the trams as they screeched round the tight corner outside the store and the noise of the wheels on the rails could be heard a few hundred yards away at least. Much quieter when it rained though. The screech of the trams, the whizz of the cash tins, the chatter of the people in the store, and the cries of the traders outside, made better music for me than the universal background tape player, that forms a part of almost every large store today.

Back again to Christmas, and the Christmas of 1938 in particular: Under the Baptist Church on the ground floor, the church hall was situated, and here they used to raise a few pounds by holding 'Bazaars' as they called them, and 'Socials' with games and dances, every month.

The money raised was used to give the poorer children of the parish a free Christmas dinner, and afterwards they played games in party hats and burst many balloons. When it was time to go home, each child was given a donated present and a net stocking containing an orange, an apple, a bar of chocolate and a shiny new penny. For many children it brought a ray of happiness into an otherwise grim and sparse existence at that time. In my mind's eye I can still see those little mites as they ran happily up the slope leading from the church hall, into the arms of their waiting mothers, their bright eyes and happy faces trying to relate everything that had happened, all in one breath and one sentence.

Sadly that Christmas of 1938 was the very last time that they ever gave that children's party.

I visited that old Baptist church a short while ago, at the bottom of Higham Hill, and it was sad to see the old place almost derelict and the old church hall is now used as commercial premises. As I stood and looked at the care worn bricks, many memories flooded back and I wondered how many times I had run up and down that slope as a child, or hidden in the boiler house at the bottom, playing 'hide and seek'. I recalled the church 'orchestra', Curly Smith on the drums, Rosie, my future mother-in-law playing the piano, her husband Reg playing the flute, and my future brother-in-law, Jack, with his violin. With a few others, they provided the music for the many Socials that Dad organised in the church hall.

A liberal scattering of French chalk on the wooden floor, made it possible to dance.

We played games, such as musical chairs, musical mat, grabbing a wife, stick in the bucket, and so on. All good clean fun, but hilarious at times too, and we really enjoyed ourselves.

In the far corner of the hall was the kitchen, with its gas fired urn for boiling water, a row of huge aluminium kettles, and stacks of thick white china cups and saucers ranged on shelves. Two butler's sinks with enormous brass taps, and a huge, scrubbed wood-topped, table completed the equipment. – 'Interval now Ladies and Gentlemen, tea is served.'

Many years later, after the war, I was home on leave from the army, and with nothing better to do I was persuaded by my mum to attend a

Saturday Social in the church hall. A very attractive A.T.S. sergeant was also there for the same reason - home on leave with nothing better to do. We met, fell in love, and were married within the year. We enjoyed the next forty happy years together.

But I am running ahead of myself - just a bit - so back to 1938 :

We had no money for grown boy's toys in the late thirties, and we made our own. A plank of wood, acquired by devious means, some old pram wheels and a soapbox were constructed to form a cart. The wooden front axle, pivoted on a single nail - or a bolt if you could scrounge one - was steered by a loop of rope or string. Straight six-inch nails were at a premium because they served as axles for the pram wheels.

With this contraption we careered down the nearest hill without brakes of any kind. Usually a wheel came off before we reached the bottom, but that was part of the fun. Getting to the bottom of the hill intact, was a bigger challenge than winning. I can remember many a torn knee and buckled wheel from carting, and a good many frightened horses, to say nothing of old ladies trying to cross the road. Wheels fell off, we fell off, but no real harm was done as the lack of traffic made the road safer than the pavement is today. It satisfied our spirit of adventure, and we had great fun scrounging the materials and building our racing carts.

Medical insurance was rare. Children received free medical treatment, but it was very basic. Dental treatment was administered from a room in the Lloyd Park building in Forest Road. As a child I had teeth pulled out under gas, which today would have been saved by a simple filling.

Before the war only the wage earners were covered by the National Insurance scheme, others had to pay or go without. Later, the Hospital Savings Association (or H.S.A.) existed to provide general hospital insurance for the less well off. I know we joined and I think Dad covered the whole family for a premium of about eight pence a week.

That eight-pence was our total outlay in insurance premiums, as nothing else was insured. Working people like us didn't have, and couldn't afford insurance, and in any case there was nothing to insure. We had no car, the house was rented, and we certainly had no possessions of value. There was always a part of the week left over at the end of the money for most households, so the insurance man stood no chance.

Pawnshops were kept busy in those days, and anything of any value could be *Popped at Uncles* when the money ran out. I can recall that Dad's best suit was good for a loan of five bob, and it cost five shillings and five pence to redeem it. Anything not redeemed within three months was put in the sale window and sold at a small profit.

Some wives made a regular trip to Uncles on a Monday morning, especially if the old man had been *on the beer* over the weekend. But this never happened to us, I am glad to say, because Dad wasn't a boozer.

Many a row ensued when a working man saw his watch, or his favourite bowler hat, offered for sale because 'The Missis' couldn't afford to get it back in time.

East End tailors used a special flat iron called a Weasel, and since they had at least two, they would Pop one of those when necessary.

'Half a pound of tuppenny rice, half a pound of treacle,
That's the way the money goes, So Pop goes the Weasel.'

Do you remember that old ditty? We used to sing it when I was very young and we played Hopscotch. We chalked numbers on the paving stones and hopped from one to the other, singing that song because it had the right rhythm.

If a child were to miss school in the morning, Mum had to send a note to the teacher via another child. If a not wasn't sent, then by the afternoon old 'Can't we have', the truant officer, would be knocking on the front door and enquiring -

'Why can't we have little Albert at school today?' When he was satisfied with the answer (and not before) he would be off on his bike to check on someone else.

He would stop any children he saw in the street during school hours, and so would the local Bobby. Playing truant was a risky business in those days because the punishment was six strokes of the cane.

My school was called the William McGuffie Boy's, in Greenleaf Road.

I attended school regularly but I was a poor scholar. The teachers did their best but I didn't learn. Teachers failed me in that they didn't make me understand <u>why</u> I needed to learn. Geography and History are of no value to me - I remember thinking - and why learn all those posh words? *Past party-sipples*, what did that mean? *First person singlar, and Split infinitives*, what was all that about? Cockney was good enough, wasn't it? With that attitude I consequently wasted my school days because I was ignorant and mentally insular, but I wasn't stupid.

Yes I blame my teachers, their first job was to teach me the value of knowledge for its own sake, and the reasons why I needed to know. Sadly, in that they failed dismally. I had left school before I understood.

The school system, in combination with the teachers - those purveyors of wisdom, those wielders of chalk, who poured knowledge into buckets with holes in them, - so often they wasted their time, and we children wasted the opportunity to learn. Even today that is much in evidence - what a waste - and how profoundly sad.

In my case the one redeeming fact was that I found Geometry and Mathematics lessons so easy that I was always finished well ahead of the class. Nevertheless, for some reason, my form master, Mr. Pettifer didn't like me, perhaps I was too cocky, I don't know, but he always resented having to mark my work 10/10 so he usually deducted a mark for neatness. He knew that I couldn't argue with that, as dirty fingers from playtime left the evidence.

It was the precision of these subjects that attracted me. There was only one correct answer, and I liked that. It could be proved, it was right, and that was that. I took to the sciences for the same reason. But in spite of my ability in the Sciences, I left school unable to spell, and with scant knowledge of the English language. It was only much later, after years of reading that my appreciation of the written word developed.

In 1938 the Extended Education Scheme was introduced whereby pupils could stay at school for an additional year to improve. But my school was not prepared for it and I wasted two terms as a general dogs-body until I left at the age of fifteen.

In 1939 Mum went away, and came back with another baby. It was to be my new brother. I was not very excited with the prospect I must admit. After all, what does a fifteen-year-old lad want with a baby brother? Babies were mother's business, so I ignored him most of the time, not his fault, but I had more important things to occupy my time.

My sister, on the other hand, was delighted and at the age of three she became his second mother. She had a real live doll to play with, what more could a girl ask for? I was happy for her, but sorry for my poor brother who had to put up with the mauling.

The district nurse was a frequent visitor to our house at this time. I was sitting on the stairs once when a pair of large legs sheathed in black lisle stockings and brogue shoes approached me, the attendant voice boomed 'Don't sit there boy it's dangerous.'

I thought that was a blooming cheek, and so after that I always said that her bicycle with its ring-ting bell was her broomstick, and her black bag was her witches cat. A childish reaction that was probably unfair, because she helped Mum a lot when she needed it most.

Now that I had left school, Dad got me an interview for a job as a telegraph boy. - Telegrams were delivered by hand in those days, by boys wearing a pillbox hat and a G.P.O. satchel, riding on a dilapidated red Post Office bicycle -

'If you get this job you will have security and a pension lad', he said.

But I wanted to be an engineer and so I purposely botched the interview. When Dad recovered he got me another interview with an electrical engineering company. It was the ASEA Electric Co. in Fulbourne Road on the corner of Forest Road. Part of it has been demolished now, and a Homebase store stands there instead.

Engineering, that was more like it, I sailed through the interview, and I gained an apprenticeship to train as a draughtsman starting when I became sixteen years of age. That was it, first foot on the ladder, so I enrolled for evening classes at the local Technical College the very next day to study for both Electrical and Mechanical engineering qualifications. A five-year course at least.

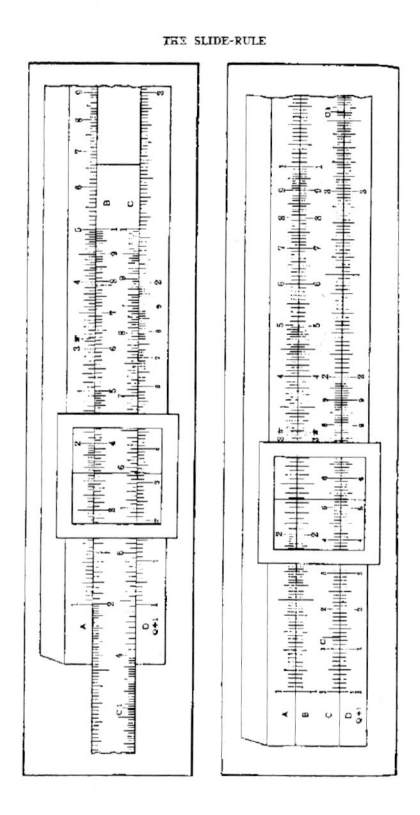

THE SLIDE-RULE

Aunt Daisy bought me a top quality slide rule for my birthday and I still have it. A slide rule is the forerunner of an electronic calculator. It is an instrument that can be used to multiply and divide to an accuracy of several decimal places if carefully used. Trigonometric and algebraic calculations can be done with it as well as normal logarithms and ordinary geometric calculations. It saved hours of laborious paper work. The only drawback was that addition and subtraction could not be done on a slide rule, and you had to keep the position of the decimal point in your head as you went along. I wonder how many slide-rules still exist today? I doubt if many people could even remember having seen one and even fewer would know how to use it.

So here I was, just fifteen years of age and not able to start my apprenticeship until I was sixteen, and the date - early in 1939.

I got a job in a factory at the top of our road, and I was assigned to a machine fixing handles onto attaché cases, but I got the sack after two weeks for *mucking about* with the other lads and girls on the assembly line.

My next job was with a butchers shop in the High Street. It wasn't much of a job. I spent most of my time delivering orders on a heavy great bike with a basket on the front. When not delivering, I had to clean up in the shop. It made Mum happy because I got plenty of cheap meat, but that didn't last, I left after a few weeks.

Next I learned to develop and print films in the local chemists in the High Street. I enjoyed that because I had an interest in photography, and also there were a lot of other lads there and I enjoyed the company.

At 3pm each day we had to do our cycle delivery round of the other chemists with the completed prints. All black and white then - no colour. The processed work was put into coded bags and each chemist had their own code letters. I used to cycle from Walthamstow as far as Woodford each day on my round and I can still remember the codes of the last six shops; YM, YR, YW, C, YF, N Exactly why I should remember those, goodness knows, but I do. If my memory was as receptive now as it was then, I would be a happier man, but sadly it gets worse with age.

My next job was at Blakey Morris the wallpaper shop in the High Street near Buxton Road. Nothing remarkable about that, but I really settled in there. I became very good friends with both Reg George the manager and his lovely wife Vera. He always called me Bert. I hated it - and Herbert - so I called myself Alby, and so it remained to this day. My name is Alby to all who know me.

Wallpaper in those days was twenty-two inches wide including a border along both edges. This border had to be trimmed off before the paper could be hung, although it was usual then to trim off only one border and to overlap one edge. The shop had a trimming machine that could cut one or both edges of the roll by the application of a hand crank. It was a bit of a Heath Robinson device but it worked reasonably well and saved a lot of work with a pair of scissors. Lining paper was priced at eight-pence, ten-pence or one shilling per roll. However there were only two qualities. Most people chose the middle priced one and they were given the eight-penny rolls, while the correct price for the shilling roll was only ten-pence. I think the difference went into our tea fund.

One day when I wanted to buy a wallpaper brush for myself, Reg said 'Buy the very best Bert, it will last you a lifetime.'
He was right, it has, I still have it and it is as good as new after sixty years of use on countless rolls of paper. The charge for trimming wallpaper was two pence per roll. Wallpapers cost from a shilling per roll, while expensive papers cost two-shillings and sixpence (Eight rolls for one pound). Imagine wallpapering a room for less than one-pound, but in those days it represented more than a day's wages.

It was the fashion then to use a heavily embossed paper below the chair rail which ran all round the room, with a patterned paper above it. The embossed paper was called Lyncrusta and it was so heavy that it required a special paste to hang it. Once hung and painted, and painted, and then repainted, it was so difficult to remove that it became a fixture. When the fashion changed years later and I removed some from our room, the plaster came off with it, and re-plastering became necessary.

Lead based paint was in common use as it was the only option for outside use against the weather. Emulsion paint was yet to be invented, and so the only choices were ready mixed oil paint, distemper, or whitewash.

Distemper by the way, was a mixture of powdered dye, size, and water so it wasn't very durable and certainly not washable.

When I finally started my engineering job, I worked all day of course, and my wages as an apprentice, were low. In the evenings I had to attend evening classes to study for my qualifications, and then revision and homework took up most of my time. At the time I remember comparing my lot with that of a close school friend. His father worked as a milkman, and he got his son a milkman's job too. My friend - my age - was given his own milk round and he was finished work by early afternoon. For that he earned a man's wages. So what was I doing working all day for a pittance and sitting in a classroom every evening? I found the answer some years later when I was earning two or three times his wage, sitting in a warm office in mid-winter.

We had a radio set at home made by Murphy, and it looked like a gothic church window made of plywood. When it was turned on, a tiny fan shaped opening lit up to illuminate the tuning dial, and the only two other controls were for the volume and tone. Hanging out at the back was the clutch of necessary batteries, attached by a bundle of wires. It was in fact quite a crude machine, but for us then we thought it was wonderful.

We had to have a massive wire aerial running the whole length of the back garden, supported by porcelain insulators on rope at each end, and situated as high as possible to pick up *the waves* for our wireless. Most Sunday mornings we would tune-in to Radio Luxembourg to listen to

Dick Barton Special Agent, and Doctor Foo-Man-Choo. Cheers for one and boos for the other.

Before television, and with no telephone of course, The radio was our only connection with the outside world. Listening to Radio Luxembourg on a Sunday morning became a ritual.

Sunday mornings too, Dad always cleaned all of the family's shoes. It was a routine for him to ensure that we all had clean shoes for church. A man of habits my dad, he liked order, and regular habits gave him a sense of security. One day when he was cleaning away on top of the coal box in the back yard, our next-door neighbour gave him a full glass of home made parsnip wine over the fence. It was a hot day and Dad drank it all. Within the hour he was *Brahms and List* and spark out on the sofa. He missed church that afternoon and he was mortified because he was due to read the lesson, and normally he never drank more than the odd beer, and he never kept any in the house.

'Just fancy old Ted missing church because he was drunk! and him a Deacon too, whatever next.' I bet he took a lot of stick over that.

Work on the Dartford tunnel under the River Thames began in 1938, but it didn't matter a jot to us, as there was no chance of us having a car to drive through it. Even a car parked in our road was a rare sight, it was probably *'the Doctor what's come to see old Mrs Wilson's leg again'.*

The Doctor would come out of the house expecting to find a row of kids sitting on the running board or on the bonnet, or checking the fixings of the spare wheel. He was rarely disappointed, and he would put his bag onto the back seat to the usual cries of;

'Give us a ride Doc. Go on, jus' t' the end of the road.' We never really expected, or received, a ride but *if you don't ask, you don't get,* and anyway *there's no harm in asking.* Petrol was one shilling and nine pence a gallon then. An old enamel sign records the fact.

Before the war, horses were still the main means of transport, and there were many concrete water troughs erected around London 'by the Metropolitan Drinking Fountain and Cattle Trough Association. The drinking fountains had a brass tap set into the stone front with an elaborately decorated push button on the front of it. A solid pewter cup was provided for use, and this was secured to the stonework by a disproportionately large chain. Personally I never used them because mum said that they were the quickest way to catch germs, and I am sure that she was right.

Some friends of Dad's had *a place in the country*. Actually it was a smallholding, and we visited them sometimes, on a Greenline Bus, out past Epping. That was quite an adventure and a delight to be *out in the fresh air* for a change. I remember the thrill of actually picking apples directly from a tree and not out of a paper bag.

I had seen big horses before, pulling brewers drays loaded with barrels of beer, but the giant country horses were something else.

On the land, before tractors took over the work, horses were used almost exclusively for mowing and ploughing, and from two to four magnificent Shire horses - depending on the size of the plough - could be seen working together as a team. That was a sight that I always enjoyed, but the skill required to drive them is now sadly becoming a past art.

Pre-war, combine harvesters had yet to become popular and mowing and threshing were done separately. After mowing, the sheaves would be carried to the side of the field to where a threshing machine would be parked. The thresher was about the size of a large removal van and powered by a huge leather belt from a separate steam engine carefully positioned in line. Farmers hired the thresher and engine by the day, much as they do today when they hire a combine harvester.

Horses were still needed however to carry coal and water to the steam engine, and to carry away the threshed corn. Farmers could grow their own fuel for horses and so they were cheap to run, tradition dies hard and horses were slow to give way to the tractor.

At the outbreak of war however, the government was making demands on the farmers for more and more food, and tractors were made available cheaply for the purpose.

As the pressure on the farming industry escalated and the increase in food production became essential, so the change over to tractors accelerated. Efficient though they are, tractors can never invoke the feelings that I have for those magnificent gentle giants.

My cousin Iris got a job in an office, training to be a Comptometer operator. If you are less than forty years old dear reader, then you will, in all probability, never have heard of a Comptometer, so I will elucidate.

A Comptometer was an electro-mechanical calculator, it was housed in a metal box approximately 30cm x 20cm and about 10cm deep.

The top carried 66 numerical typewriter keys in seven vertical rows of nine, with three extra. On the right hand side a crank lever operated the mechanism. Large offices would have a room full of operators performing calculating miracles at rapid speed. Some girls were highly skilled and their speed and accuracy was much prized.

The Comptometer remained the basic tool of accountants and banks for over sixty years, until the electronic calculator gradually replaced it in the 1970's. Today Iris would have trained on a computer keyboard, but in those days it was the Comptometer Operators and Shorthand Typists that kept commerce functioning.

The first inclination of an impending war came in September 1938, when Chamberlain returned from Germany declaring 'Peace with Honour' but very few people actually believed that Hitler would keep to his assurances. In that year also I saw my first ever Barrage Balloon when they were demonstrated down at Kidbrooke, just south of the Thames.

I didn't know then just how familiar they were to become. The Munich scare of 1938 started preliminary war preparations that were to stand us in good stead a year later.

Recruiting for the three services began also in 1938 and a surge of young men applied to become airforce pilots. During the early days of 1939 I remember seeing swarms of biplanes in the sky as the pilots trained hard and honed their skills for the coming conflict.

When Christmas came in 1938 most people forgot all about Germany. Auntie Edie took me to see Father Christmas at Selfridges in

London, and afterwards to see the pantomime Dick Whittington, and finally to tea in Lyons Corner House. That was to be the last time that she took me on that annual treat, but I remember it, every bit of it, and her kindness too, God bless her.

On that day early in December, London was covered in a thick fog. But there was nothing unusual about that as more often than not, it was foggy in London. I have known fogs so thick that it was impossible to see beyond an outstretched arm. These fogs formed from chimney smoke, as it became trapped in stagnant sulphur laden air. The result was a choking, eye watering, mouth clogging, impenetrable yellow smog.

It was, without a doubt, a killer, and any poor soul with Tuberculosis or other lung problems didn't stand a chance. Everything that you touched left a black streak of soot, and when you blew your nose, the handkerchief became covered in soot. It was like living in a chimney.

On this occasion though, it wasn't too bad, as it was just possible to see across the road, and the Christmas lights of Regent Street and Oxford Street, made it a lot easier to move around. The fog gave an eerie atmosphere to everything, as people materialised out of the mist only to disappear again, like ghosts. I held on tightly to Auntie Edie with one hand, and to my present from Santa with the other, even though I was now a big boy of fourteen.

In the new-year there was a lot of talk, and reports in the papers, about a possible war, but nobody seemed very worried at the prospect, and the general attitude seemed to be one of stoical acceptance. *Be all over in six months mate*, was the general opinion.

The summer of 1939 passed quietly enough, Prime Minister Nevil Chamberlain and the King made a few speeches on the wireless, and the papers talked of *a gathering storm.*
I was now fifteen and in my overrun year at school, so I was the Indian Chief in the school playground hierarchy. I was still a boy, but soon to grow up rapidly, as war was about to consume all of my teenage years.

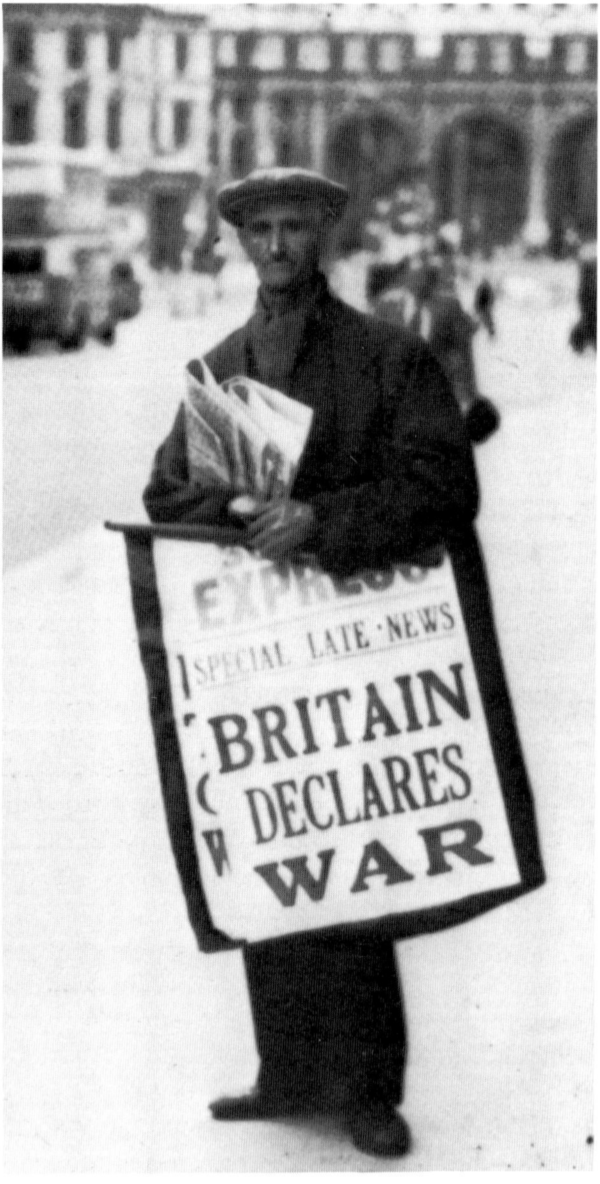
EXPRESS
SPECIAL LATE NEWS
BRITAIN
DECLARES
WAR

1939 - 1946

September came in 1939 and our lives were to change beyond anything that we could have imagined, never to be the same again - for the survivors that is, for many were soon to die.

Neither I, nor anyone else knew what we were in for on that fateful Sunday as we listened to the announcement on the wireless. In my ignorance I accepted the news with some excitement, but my parents knew better, they had already lived through one war.

Although war was officially declared on September the third, the authorities knew long before, that war was inevitable, and preparations had been well underway for many months since the Munich scare of a year earlier.

During the first weeks of September 1939, almost one and a half million mothers and children were evacuated from London, and many kids were to see the real countryside for the first time.

Not many mothers were evacuated, mostly teachers, as whole schools were moved *en bloc*. The evacuees were not told where they were going and groups of bewildered children could be seen waiting for busses or trains to whisk them off to *God knows where*. They stood tearfully in their best outfits, with a change of clothes and night wear in a bag or suitcase. They each wore a large luggage label bearing their name, address and school, tied on a piece of string round their neck, with a gas mask in its regulation cardboard box slung over one shoulder. Some had a cricket bat or a teddy bear tucked under one arm, but all had that baffled uncomprehending look on their faces, and their eyes asked 'Why?'

Mums and Dads, eyes full of tears, tried not to give in to crying as they had their last desperate hug from children hanging out of windows, as the train started to move. None of them knew at that moment when they would see each other again.

Thousands more of them were to leave London before Christmas, leaving behind tearful parents anxiously awaiting the first postcard to tell them where their offspring had gone. Most of the evacuees were lucky and found loving and understanding homes, but a few were simply used as unpaid servants and found an environment of drudgery.

Later when the first rush had died down and things were sorted out, the unlucky ones were rescued and moved to more congenial surroundings. Some simply couldn't settle into a new life, and they dribbled back to London and the roulette of life in the Blitz.

Conscription plans were already made and the first 'call-up' papers were served on men between the ages of eighteen and forty one, for the various armed forces.

Anderson bomb shelters were issued in London, and families with an income below £250 a year got one free, I'm sure we didn't pay for ours

Dad and I dug a hole over a metre deep in our back garden, 'as far as possible from a building' the instructions said. Dad laid a concrete base on a layer of rubble, and we erected the corrugated iron sections on top of that. When they were all securely bolted together we built a twin wall of sand, or rather earth bags, all around it and then filled in the top with more earth packed down hard. Another layer of sandbags was firmly rammed in position on top of that.

A small opening about 60 X 80cm was left at one end for access, and we protected this with a right angled wall of sandbags. Next we installed two wooden bunks with wire netting to support the mattress, a small table, and a paraffin lantern completed the essentials.

We criss-crossed our windows with yard upon yard of sticky brown paper tape, to reduce the risk of flying glass, and black-out curtains or screens were improvised for all windows. Outside doors were hung with heavy curtains to form light traps, and my London prepared for war.

In May 1940 the Local Defence Volunteers were formed, later to become the Home Guard. Men between the ages of 18 and 65 were required to join, but in those early days it was very rudimentary, as there was only one rifle for every ten men, and very few uniforms. Dad was given a gun and a bayonet, but no ammunition. The groups of men that met in the local school, had a long way to go in their training before they would become an effective force. They took a lot of stick in those early days, and they were the butt of many jokes. Most men armed themselves with shotguns that appeared from nowhere, the rest drilled with broomsticks.

Over a million men joined The Home Guard in the first six weeks, half of whom had served in the First World War.

It is not my intention here to recount the history of the war - far from it - I am simply trying to paint the back-cloth and set the scene as it were, as far as it affected me and my family. We were however all similar players in the same drama that was to be everyone's experience during *the blitz* as London fought for its survival.

My own experiences are just a small sample of what thousands of Londoners lived through, but I relate them because being first hand, they may have some value.

It was about this time in my life that I began to be conscious of people as individuals rather than just beings. That is to say that I began to look upon other people with an adult outlook. Whereas previously I had viewed them dispassionately as objects, I now became aware of them as personalities. I began to realise for the first time that each one had their own personal problems, hopes, and fears, and that they were moved and motivated by their own aspirations. Previously they had simply been - in my childish mind - people who were just *there*, on the fringe of my own interests. Now I began to see them as separate entities, and in consequence each one became infinitely more interesting.

At the age of fifteen years and eight months, I joined the A.R.P. (Air Raid Precautions) and became an Air Raid Warden. We were issued with a tin hat, a stirrup pump, and an armband, and a leaflet written by someone with no more experience of air-raids than we had ourselves.

Warden's posts were established in any suitable shelter - a garage, or a shed, or a derelict van parked at the end of the street. Later the Local Council built small brick shelters with a steel covered roof, and a steel door. A bit of a waste of time really since when there was a raid in progress, we were out and about doing our job. We only used the post to house a telephone, and to shelter from the rain between raids, Oh yes, and to make the tea.

There were five or six wardens in our post, with one post to every five hundred people. Our badge of office was a yellow armband.

The familiar blue battle-dress was issued much later, when the A.R.P. became the Civil Defence Corps. In the early days all we had to do was to patrol our area, check the blackout precautions, top up the fire buckets at fire points, and help the old folks to the shelters.

After all the hurried and fervent preparations nothing happened, and we wondered what the fuss had been about.

We had a quiet year (the phoney war) until the air raids began in earnest in September 1940 - then we found out - and we discovered the real meaning of *hell on earth*.

In that year also I had all the odd jobs that I have previously mentioned, in the run up to starting my apprenticeship and serious employment.

For the population of England, that quiet year proved to be vitally important however, because in September 1939 we were totally unprepared for what was to happen in September 1940. That year gave us time to train and to get things organised, albeit in ignorance of the true horrors to come.

By September 1940, I had transferred to the Heavy Rescue Service, (C.D.Rescue) and that was my job throughout the Blitz. In writing this, many horrific images come to mind that I would rather forget, but it is necessary to refer to some of them in order to tell the story.

I will however gloss over the details, as this is not a horror story. I was very lucky, I survived completely unscathed, but sadly many thousands did not. The casualty totals are almost unreal and unbelievable in hindsight.

In eight months from September 1940 to May 1941 over 20,000 Londoners lost their lives, and some 70,000 were injured. On Saturday the 9th of September a series of intensive raids on London's Docks began, Surrey Docks, Millwall, Isle of Dogs, - all of them - and 1500 people were killed in the fist four days. How can you prepare for that?

Westminster Abbey, The House of Commons, The Tower of London were all bombed in May 1941. So was my aunt and our neighbours in the next street and one of our Wardens.

One night during an early air raid, I was out on duty, when my head suddenly exploded, and I fell to the ground. A colleague was with me and he brought me round. A piece of shrapnel from an anti-aircraft shell had fallen to earth and pierced my tin helmet. Fortunately there is a space between the metal and the skull, and the shrapnel had penetrated only far enough to break the skin on my head. What a lucky escape that was.

It adds truth to the saying that 'Only the good die young'. That helmet hung in our rescue centre throughout the war to remind everyone to wear theirs. I'm glad I did.

One weekend there was a daytime raid and aircraft could be heard overhead. Dad was undressed for some reason so he dressed quickly and took mum and the family down to our shelter. It was a long raid and there were no toilet facilities in our small shelter of course, so Dad popped out to water the roses. Mum heard him cursing and grumbling and he returned to the shelter very flustered.

'What's up'? asked Mum.

'Put me damned pants on back to front didn't I ?' replied Dad.

Initially it was intended that the rescue services would stay in their allocated areas, but very soon the bombing became so intense, especially towards the city and the docks, that we rushed in lorries with our gear, to wherever we could do the most good.

One night we were called to help at a major incident in Leyton, a neighbouring borough, where a stick of heavy bombs had left a string of devastation. In one house a birthday party had been in full swing when they got a direct hit in their back yard. We were digging one young chap out, and as I pulled on his arms to drag him clear only his top half came free, but we got a young girl out alive missing one arm, she was crying, and managed to say,

'My arm is broken I think.'

I suppose she was lucky - if it can be called luck - life or death, it's all relative I suppose, because surviving or dying was considered to be purely a matter of luck.

'If it's got yer name on it mate, - that's it.'

Ambulances were kept busy ferrying the non-life-threatening injured to the first aid posts and the seriously injured to hospital, picking their way cautiously around the debris and through the broken glass that was strewn everywhere. The dead were placed on flat backed lorries and tied with a label giving as much information as was known, such as the name of the road and the approximate house number where they were found, for transfer straight to the many temporary morgues in use at that time.

It never occurred to me that one night I could be one of them. It all seemed so unreal, as if it was all going on in spite of me and I was remote from it just an onlooker. And yet I wasn't of course, I was very much involved, but at the same time, and in a strange way, I felt immune from the obvious dangers.

One night a very excited lady rushed into a Wardens Post when I was there and she stammered;
'A bomb - there's a bomb - in the road it is - it's big - right in the middle of the road - come see.'
So we went to see, and she was right. At the top end of our road, right in the middle was a bomb, but we could only see the top half of it. There it was, a medium sized normal bomb of about 250lbs. that had scored a bulls-eye on a circular manhole cover, and it was now firmly wedged into the manhole like a boiled egg in an eggcup.
The bomb disposal squad had one hell of a job removing it, and in the end they took it away complete with a manhole collar still firmly fixed around it. Apparently it had not exploded because the nose cone had not been hit hard enough, either that or it was a dud.

After one particular raid I was near to a friends house that had been damaged by blast. I went looking for him and I walked through to their Anderson shelter in the back garden.
'Are you O.K.' I called out.
'Yes love' his mum said, 'let yourself in, I'm coming up, the key is under the front doormat.' I burst out laughing and called back ;
'I'm already in ma', your front door is half way up the hall and the mat is on the stairs.'
At another incident, I was helping to tunnel under a collapsed building to get some people out from the basement, when I became aware of an RAF chap beside me helping in the rescue. He was covered from head to toe in dirt and dust like the rest of us, and he was telling me as we worked that he was on leave and he had left his wife in the shelter with her parents.
When we eventually reached some women and children and got them out, two women and one child were injured. The airman was angry and emotional as he said
'At least in the forces we can fight back, these people are the real heroes.'

As the dust cleared I saw a pair of trouser clad legs sticking out from a pile of loose rubble, so I set to and got the person out quite quickly. He wasn't hurt and as I helped him to his feet I said

'You'll be O.K. now son.' The dirt engrained face turned to me, smiled, and two twinkling eyes said;

'Son be damned, I'm eighteen, and a girl, can't you tell?' Then she kissed me and we both fell about laughing. I never saw her again.

In the area after bombs had fallen, and with the coming of daylight, all kinds of things could be seen hanging from the trees in the road, making them look like scruffy Xmas trees. Stuck in the branches or hanging from telegraph poles were personal things, like underclothes and bedding, pieces of paper, an open umbrella pierced by a branch, a shirt or a bra, all strewn about no longer personal but very public.

People became like that when they slept together cheek by jowl on a cold underground station platform. Starting as strangers initially, as dissimilar as an umbrella and a bra, drawn together on the same tree of necessity - together - comforting each other in adversity, and in the morning, strangers no longer. Yet with the coming of another day they parted, each to their own purpose, perhaps to survive or maybe to become a victim in a later incident.

The morning after a heavy raid was a weird time. People in their office suits were trying as best they could to get to work. Firemen were damping down the few remaining fires still smouldering and rolling up their hoses. Milkmen could be seen looking at the remains of houses and crossing off the order in their book, with no chance of recovering the unpaid bill.

Pieces of charred paper floated about in a light wind, while people with nothing but the night clothes they stood in, wandered about like lost souls in a state of shock, wondering what to do next.

What do you do next, when your home is a pile of rubble?

The emergency services were swamped and had probably asked them to come back later in the day. Others, lucky enough to have a few salvaged possessions in hastily grabbed bags, made their way to the station or bus stop in the hope of finding a bed with friends or relatives. Destitute and homeless, and yet they were the lucky ones who were still alive, as I said, it's all relative.

In Tottenham in north London a large park had been turned over to allotments until the local council decided to build a very large air raid shelter on the land. Everyone local was delighted with the idea, as it was very much needed, and the local paper, The Guardian, announced that the grand opening was to be performed by the Mayor with a local band in attendance.

The night following the opening, the new shelter was full, when it received a direct hit by a 1,000 lb. bomb. There were so many killed that it was impossible to dig them all out or to piece together the bodies. Consequently the Council had to ask neighbours to report any empty houses, or anyone that had not been seen around for a while, in an attempt to compile a casualty list.

Elsewhere so many families had been bombed out of their homes, that the relief centres were full. People were forced to try to survive and live wherever shelter could be found. Schools, left empty by the evacuees, were soon full, as were the churches, warehouses, stations, etc. Hundreds of East-Enders took up permanent residence in the underground tube stations, and some of them regularly bought a platform ticket every day so that they couldn't be legally removed.

The transport officials finally gave in, and they painted a white line along the platform half way between the wall and the platform edge. Wall to the line - for public shelter, and line to the edge - kept clear for travellers.

After the last train of the night had passed, the line was crossed until the morning rush started again. It was a system that worked well for all concerned.

It was around Christmas 1940, as far as I can remember, that the Luftwaffe started dropping mines. These were flat-ended canisters, about the size of two oil-drums end to end, and they floated down on a huge parachute. They were set to explode at a low altitude so that the blast would cause greater devastation. Fortunately some of them failed to go off and could be seen hanging from trees or high buildings. I remember seeing one dangling from the spire of St.John's church in Palmerston Road.

Special bomb disposal squads from the Royal Engineers became experts in defusing these devices together with ordinary unexploded bombs.

The bombs made safe enough to move were usually taken to Hackney Marshes where they were safely exploded. It was not at all unusual to see an open lorry with red painted mudguards, and UXB painted on the sides, dashing along with horn blaring and a huge bomb on the back, sandbags along each side to stop it rolling, with two or three Royal Engineers sitting astride it, as it was taken to be destroyed.

Some of the larger bombs weighing 500lbs. or 1000lbs., that could not be safely moved, were sometimes blown up on site after a hurried evacuation of nearby residents. Later they hit upon the idea of using a steam pipe to wash out the explosive on the big ones. This avoided the need to blow them up, and saved a lot of extra damage.

The bomb disposal engineers were the real heroes of the blitz, it takes guts and cool courage to sit astride a ticking 500lb bomb and calmly work on removing its fuse before it blows up and removes you first.

Some of these wonderful chaps were killed, but they saved the lives of hundreds of people who never knew them, and who were never able to express their gratitude.

Earlier I mentioned a Stirrup Pump. Perhaps I had better elucidate for younger readers; A stirrup pump was like a bicycle pump on a bracket. The pump was dropped into a bucket of water, with the bracket outside. One foot on the bracket base steadied the pump, whilst you pumped like mad to send the water along a half inch rubber hose-pipe.

With this contraption we were expected to tackle fires started by incendiary bombs. But mostly they were used for watering the garden or spraying the roses, since water sprayed onto burning magnesium only made things worse, like petrol on a bonfire.

Incendiary bombs were quite small, about the size of a lemonade bottle, and as you would expect they landed mostly on roofs. Those that landed on the ground, we ignored.

Can you imagine standing on a ladder with a bucket of water and a stirrup pump? Not a silly question, because if the bucket was left down on the ground, it was almost impossible to pump sufficient pressure for an effective jet, two storeys or more high up on the roof of a house.

They were of use psychologically though, because at least you had something to fight back with, and sometimes they were found to be effective on secondary fires.

We hit on the idea of using a long pole with a hook on the end. With this we would hook the fin of the bomb and drop it into the garden where it could burn itself to death. Incendiaries were always dropped in clusters anyway, so you had to be quick with each one until they had all been tackled.

Sometimes they broke through the roof tiles and started fires in the loft space. These were very difficult to detect until they had actually started a fire and produced a smoke signal. We found that the most effective method was to dump a bucket of sand on the magnesium incendiary, and then to attack the fire with water.

Later in the war, incendiary bombs were fitted with anti-personnel explosive, a bit like a small land mine, so that when touched they would blow your hand or head off. They were very tricky to deal with. We used to try to drop a lasso of rope over them and then to set them off from a safe distance.

When the raids were long and heavy, with intensive incendiary bombing, most of the water main's got broken. So that meant there was insufficient water available to fight the intensive fires. When that happened, water was drawn from the Thames or the river Lee.

Away from the rivers, large steel water tanks had been built on any spare piece of land for this contingency, and they proved to be invaluable in saving many properties from complete destruction.

Mobile anti aircraft guns were used in 1940 and these were mounted on railway trucks and shunted along to wherever they could be most useful. These were quick firing automatic cannon, nicknamed Pom-poms. At the bottom of Somers road, at the junction with Palmerstone Road, a railway line passes beneath the road level. Often these Pom-pom guns would park there, because the space between the' bridges offered good shelter for them, but the noise was deafening as we were above the level of the gun's muzzles. It was reassuring though to see the spaced tracer shells hitting back for us.

By October 1940 - that is in the <u>first two months</u> of *the Blitz*, a quarter of a million Londoners had been made homeless by the bombing.

On the 29th of December 1940, the Bank Station on the London underground suffered a direct hit from a large bomb, and over 100 people (reported 115) sheltering there were killed and many others were injured.

January 1941 came eventually, and with it my seventeenth birthday. The weather turned really foul in the new-year, and it added to the misery of those families that had had their roofs damaged and their windows blown out. But it also kept the Luftwaffe away, as the weather was too bad for flying.

During the respite, London had time to recover a little and many improvements were made. New water mains were laid and broken ones repaired, shelters were reinforced and fitted with proper toilets. Bunk beds were installed in many shelters, houses were patched up and a degree of normality - if it could be called that - was restored.

Unfortunately the lull didn't last for long, because as the weather improved, gradually the raids increased in volume and by the 19th March they were back in earnest and another 750 Londoners died in that single night. Stop a minute to think of it - 750 - a number you read and pass over, but today if 100 or so people are killed in an accident it is reported as a disaster, - and so it is, to be sure. - But during the war, 750 in one night, and more the next night, and the next, on and on for months…
I just wanted you to see it in context.

Yet worse was to come, the heavy raids continued and on the devastating night of the 10th May 1941, there were another 1,500 people killed in and around London. It was the largest number of fatalities in any single night-time raid of the war. Fortunately it proved to be the last of the major raids, and from that point London started to recover from its injuries.

That was just as well because the inhabitants were almost at breaking point. We were close to the limits that even the Cockney spirit and the British resolve could absorb. We had taken so much punishment that everyone was nearly exhausted.

In addition to those killed, many thousands were injured, and thousands more lost everything that they owned. On top of all the air raids and the consequent destruction, the people also had to cope with rationing.

Petrol had already been rationed since 23rd. September 1939, but without a car that didn't bother our family very much, but paraffin for our heating stove became hard to get and on the 8th January 1940 - butter, sugar, ham and bacon, were rationed.

We got only 4 ozs per week of butter, and 4ozs of ham or bacon. The sugar ration was 12 ozs per week, but that wasn't bad, because if someone in the family didn't take sugar in their tea it was enough to manage on.

Meat was rationed in March 1940 by price. The cheaper the cut the more you got.

My first serious attempt at education began in September 1939 when my first session of evening classes began at the South West Essex Technical College. I was determined not to waste this opportunity, and it was to take me four years to obtain an H.N.C. qualification in both electrical and mechanical engineering.

In February 1940 I started my apprenticeship at the A.S.E.A. Electric Company, ultimately to become a draughtsman. But I had to spend six months in various departments to *learn the ropes*. I started off in the assembly shop where the huge power transformers were built. The larger ones were massive and we had to use scaffolding to reach the top of them.

Two inch diameter steel bolts held the laminations together and two of us had to lean on the enormous spanner to tighten the nuts.

These big transformers were enclosed in steel cases, and then they were filled with mineral oil for insulation and cooling. German fighters made a habit of machine gunning electrical installations, and so we often had transformers returned for repair. Everything that we touched was coated in slippery oil and I went home soaked in the stuff. We dug squashed bullets out of the windings sometimes but mostly they were fused out of existence.

We were happy to think that these bullets had been used up on a transformer, we could repair that, and they hadn't killed anyone.

From July 1940, tea, cooking fats, jam & cheese were also rationed. Eggs and milk were allocated to shops in proportion to the number of customers registered with them.

We normally got one egg per fortnight if we were lucky, but it was not guaranteed. Dad kept chickens in the back yard so we were OK. Cereals, biscuits, tinned fruit and fish, were on a points system and people could choose what they wanted to buy, up to their allocation of points.

Later on a typical week's ration around the middle of the war was ;
2.oz.Tea: 8.oz.Sugar: 4.oz.Jam: 3.oz.Sweets: 2.oz.Lard: 2.oz.Marg
2.oz.Butter:4.oz.Cheese: 4.oz.Bacon: 3/4.lb.Meat; and 1 fresh Egg if you could get one. (One third of a kilo of meat for a whole week.)

Dried egg powder was the only alternative, this had to be reconstituted - 1 teaspoon of dried egg, plus two teaspoons of water = 1 egg.

Many ingenious recipes were concocted using dried eggs and other food substitutes. Many of them were very good too. Dried egg omelette and Spam fritters became the usual fall back meal.

Tons of Spam from America, became, in the second World War, as Corned Beef was during the First. It was the staple tinned meat, I liked it.

Eating out was restricted, and the official maximum cost of a meal was set at five shillings. Chinese nosh was by far the best fill-up for five bob.

Really good news was a notice in the butcher's which read;
' A full meat ration available this week.'
Rationing was popular because it was fair and everyone shared equally in what was available. We were all in it together, pulling together to survive and determined to win. Sometimes housewives shouted at the butcher if they thought that he was being unfair in his distribution of sausages, which were off ration. When a housewife bought her meat ration it had to be good stuff, and so scraps of meat went into the sausages. We ate loads of sausage toad in the hole.

By the end of 1941 the raids had begun to ease off a bit, especially at night-time, and daylight raids took their place. We thought that was the beginning of the end of the Blitzkrieg, but we didn't know then that the V1s and the V2s were yet to come.

Things were fairly quiet for a while - relatively quiet that is - as air raids continued but not with the previous intensity. Life returned to wearisome wartime normality. I saved up my clothing coupons for a badly needed suit, because I had finally reached the hallowed drawing office as a trainee.

It was possible then to buy a new suit at the Fifty Bob Tailors (that is two pounds ten shillings) but I was gangly and *off the peg* didn't fit me. So I had mine made to measure.- there's posh!

There was a bespoke tailors in Hoe Street and Old Mr Watts (he was old to me then) was the archetypal genuine master tailor who did everything by hand, from the cutting of a suit to the fitting and making up. (He gave me a pair of tailor's shears, which I still have and use.) His son John, who managed the shop, became a close friend of mine after I started to work in the shop at weekends. John was genuinely flat footed, and so he was rejected for call up into the forces. This was long after I had started my apprenticeship.

He had a Morris 10, saloon car and he taught me to drive it. His father lived in the country, in Ongar, Essex. We often drove down there on Sundays, and it was there that I learned to use a shotgun. I always came home with at least one rabbit.

One day we were driving along the Essex road, all by ourselves when a car wheel bowled up alongside of us, it overtook us, and we watched it bounce over a low hedge and disappear across a field. John said

'Some poor sod has lost a wheel'.

It was then that we realised that we were alone, it was one of our wheels! I was driving, so I gently slowed to a stop, and then, and only then, the car tipped slowly onto its rear brake drum. We retrieved the wheel but where were the nuts? So we took one nut from each of the other wheels, put the miscreant back in place, and continued our journey as if nothing had happened.

We were lucky not to have finished up in the ditch.

I always enjoyed those trips out to Ongar because we ate well for one thing. Country folk always had plenty of vegetables and eggs, with chickens and rabbits, and ham, to say nothing of the odd lamb slaughtered on the quiet. Added to all that, John had a cousin who always came with us, she was a lovely girl of my own age. We didn't exactly fall in love, but we were very fond of each other, and so that added extra excitement to our weekends in the country.

The family called her Joanna, but I called her Jo-jo.

Haystacks, quiet country lanes, back of the car in the dark coming home late on Sunday nights, we had plenty of chances to be alone. Needless to say we took full advantage of the situation, accompanied with a nod and a wink from the older generation.

I learned to drive a tractor to cut the hay, how to build a haystack, how to ride a horse, how to clean and skin a rabbit, how to toss a hay bale, oh so many skills were learned during my trips to Ongar. And Jo-jo taught me a few things as well.

Monday mornings found us back in the real world, to discover possibly that someone you knew had been bombed and killed over the weekend. A tragedy, such as that was simply accepted as a fact, not callously, but as a normal event to be expected at any time. General conversation included talk of friends who had died or lost their homes, or of relations missing after an air raid. Death became an everyday normality. War was happening everywhere, overseas, in the next town, in the next street, it was all around us. Tragedy, and injury, and death, were literally on our doorstep.

By this time we had become so inured to being bombed and possible death, that we seldom used our shelters. The attitude was that if it has got your name on it, it will find you - in the shelter or not - so we slept comfortably in our beds and ***took our chances.***

One idle Saturday morning I found that I still had an unused twelve-bore cartridge in my coat pocket. As I wandered around our back garden wondering what to do with it, I noticed that our clothesline post was adjustable for height. That meant that it had a row of holes drilled in the post so that a peg could be pushed in to adjust the post height.

The twelve-bore cartridge fitted exactly into one of these holes. The brass cap now looked me straight in the eye, daring me to do something about it. So I got a poker and a hammer and fired the damn thing that had been teasing me. I don't know what possessed me to do that, but having done it there was no going back.

We lived in a row of back to back terraced houses, so the end of our garden was also the end of the garden of the house in the next street. The lady that lived there had a line of washing out, and this now hung in tatters as the shot had torn down the line ripping her washing to shreds.

What had got into me? What a bloody stupid thing to have done! Aghast - I ran indoors only to find that the cartridge case had blown back, the length of our garden, and it had broken our kitchen window. It lay there accusingly on the kitchen floor amidst a shower of glass.

Oh, my gaud! What would Mum say when she came home? I picked up the cartridge and ran, up the passage, out of the front door, ran down the alley, ran across the market, up the road, and I didn't stop running until I got to the Hollow Pond in Epping Forest where I sat trembling on a fallen log.

Eventually when I calmed down I started to think - What was the evidence? Torn washing and a broken window, nothing else, I had the spent cartridge in my pocket. I felt safer after I had I thrown the cartridge and watched it sink slowly into a stagnant pond.

What else? Everyone at home had been out, and if I hadn't shot the lady at the back, she must have been out too. Our garden fence was high so I was unlikely to have been seen by a neighbour. Who knows that it was me then? and bangs were commonplace

It view of the dire consequences of owning up, and the fact that it wouldn't do anyone any good anyway, I finally decided that I knew nothing whatsoever about it.

Feeling a lot calmer, I wandered about for a while, and returned home via the market two hours later. To the inevitable question of;

'What do you know about this' I had my prepared answer ready,

'Know about what Mum?' It was easier to plead total ignorance, rather than to have to provide a lying alibi. The neighbours were gathered over the fence all offering various possibilities for the damage, and I think they agreed that it must have been bullets from an aerial dogfight as German fighters had been seen that very afternoon. I really did enjoy listening to all the many explanations, as only I knew the truth. Looking back with the wisdom and serenity of age, I think I must have been a right little sod.

Our neighbour put in a claim for war damage and was allocated a stack of clothing coupons, so she was happy.

During the Blitz, I would cycle to work, weaving around the piles of broken glass and debris that littered the roads first thing in the morning after a raid. Punctures were frequent and puncture repair outfits were at a premium, whilst new tyres and inner-tubes were almost impossible to obtain.

I was also attending evening classes, but air raids made evening study impractical, so we were allowed one day off work each week to attend day courses. This worked extremely well and I managed to achieve good results. I knew at long last why I needed to know, I wanted to know, and I learned. - Better late than never.

I was working as a draughtsman by day, studying after tea until the sirens sounded, then on rescue duty until the all clear finally allowed fretful sleep in the early hours of the morning. I often overslept and was late for work, but at least I had had a few hours in my own bed.

Being late in the mornings was accepted, as we were all relieved in the drawing office when a colleague finally arrived to take his place at his desk. Two of the drawing boards stood empty and unoccupied already.

Sometimes on Saturdays I helped the milkman on his rounds, he served milk straight from the churn then, measured with a dipper on a long handle, and tipped straight into he customer's jug. Woolworths sold circular rubber heels to repair boots. Do you remember? They had a star shaped washer in the middle and a single screw in the centre so that the heel could be turned round as it wore away. Anyway, one of these rubber heels, washer removed, was found to be a snug fit into the bottom of the one-pint dipper. Consequently customers got a quarter of an inch less milk in their measure and Milkie pocketed the difference.

He carried half a dozen churns on a small flat-backed, horse drawn cart. His horse was called Charlie, after Charlie Dilkie, (whoever he was!) and that is Cockney rhyming slang for Milkie or Milkman. Both Charlie and the milkman were killed later during an early morning air raid.

People who had a garden had been given Anderson shelters, and those who lived in flats were issued with Morrison shelters. These were double bed sized tables made of steel girders with a leg in each corner. They had a steel plate over the top and heavy wire mesh fitted round the sides. A mattress and bedding placed inside provided a protected place to sleep.

These were fine if placed on a solid concrete floor, but on floorboards the protection was more psychological than practical, because under a few tons of rubble, the legs would punch through the floor and the occupants became the filling in a sandwich.

Chimney stacks - that large chunk of masonry perched high on the roof - did untold damage because they were easily dislodged by bomb vibrations, and the solid mass crashed down, smashing through floor joists as it fell. One six-chimney stack from a three-storey house smashed down and landed on a Morrison shelter in the basement. The shelter folded in the centre like a half open book. Sadly a couple of old folks were sleeping there, my mates and I dug down to retrieve the four pieces.

The Women's Volunteer Service (W.V.S.) were marvellous. Whenever there was an incident, there they were, in their green van, dispensing tea and dry bread sandwiches to all in need. After the above trauma, we went for a mug of tea to clear our throats. I was handed a sandwich and in the dark I bit into it. It was sardines in oil, just what I needed, and I threw up into someone's privet hedge.

It wasn't all bad, we had many successes, more often than not the people we dug out were alive, some injured, but a large proportion made a full recovery.

The spirit and fortitude of those East-Enders is something I found inspiring. Whatever they endured, they came back for more with a smile and a joke, undaunted and determined not to be beaten. A shop with the front blown out and glass everywhere carried a rough sign which said 'More open than usual'.

We lived in a long row of terraced houses, in regimented streets with back to back gardens. Early one morning a small bomb, from a fighter bomber, dropped half way up the next street behind us. It neatly demolished two adjoining houses at the dividing walls as though workmen had done it with care. One was empty, but the old lady who lived next-door with her three cats was not so lucky. On the dividing wall left standing, I saw a polished piece of wood holding a row of brass hooks. Three matching china jugs hung there in perfect condition, but all the walls and floors had gone leaving just the blank wall, the three jugs, and a piece of flapping wallpaper blowing in the slight wind.

One evening we heard the bombers overhead a good half an hour before Wailing Winnie made the raid official. I was on my way to report for duty when I heard the scream of falling bombs. By then we could tell the difference between bombs about to fall on you, and those which were at a safe distance.

These meant business, so I threw myself full length against a front garden wall, with my face down, and my tin hat on the back of my head. As a stick of bombs fell, I heard crump, crump, crump, the blast of the nearest one tore over my back, and I felt the earth heave.

I got up unhurt and ran towards the familiar cloud of dust. As it cleared I saw the crater in the centre of the road spewing water from a broken main. The bomb was fortunately a small one, but it had demolished the front half of the house nearest to me. I looked up to see that the stairs and the walls had gone as far back as the bathroom. Sitting there on the toilet was an old chap with his trousers round his ankles.

He saw me and called out:

'Ow the 'ell do I git darn from 'ere son?' I called back,

'You'll fall down dad if you don't sit very still, hang on while I get a ladder.' As I turned away I heard him say;

'Wish I 'ad a camera. This'll give the missis a laugh.'

But it didn't, as we found her later under a ton or two of rubble.

The smell of plaster and brick dust, mixed with coal gas, haunts me still. Sometimes, if I catch the smell of a coal fire, the images come flooding back as if it were only last year.

Fortunately coal gas is lighter than air and it soon clears in the wind, so the chance of a gas explosion was greatly reduced. Burst water mains, on the other hand, were a big problem, not only because of the lack of pressure to fight fires, but sometimes people sheltering in their cellars were drowned before we could dig down to get them out.

When a water stopcock is buried under half a house, finding it simply takes too long, it is quicker to dig down to the cellar. Only very rarely were we too late.

In the areas of high rise flats, public shelters were built on any open space at ground level. These were built very substantially and saved lots of lives. They were protection against everything except a direct hit.

One night, I was in Leytonstone coming home on my bike, when the sirens sounded a bit earlier that usual. I peddled faster in order to get back to report for duty, and I could hear the heavy bombers already overhead.

Above the drone I heard the growing sound of falling bombs, so I got off the bike and stood in the shelter of a wall. I could see down a side street and I watched as people rushed to get into the shelter at the bottom. They were mothers and children mostly, and lots of older folks, all desperately dashing to get into the shelter. Children were hastily grabbed from their prams and carried, and a helping hand was given to an old lady with a stick.

A warden was there guiding and assisting, and some workmen carried the younger children, as they all hastened to get under cover.

A huge explosion not far away, was followed by another a bit closer, and my instinct took over. I flattened myself down against the wall, lying full length with my arms over my head, and waited.

I didn't have to wait long before an almighty blast seemed to lift the earth and me with it, before slamming me down again. It felt as if someone had opened the door of a huge oven, and I could hardly breathe. I opened one eye to find the air thick with dust like a fog and I couldn't see a thing.

I realised then that I wasn't hurt, and a sense of relief flooded over me, so I lay still for a few moments while my nerves returned to normal and the adrenalin rush subsided. I got to my feet and looked round the corner and down the side-street towards the shelter - It wasn't there!

Thinking that I had turned round, I turned to look the other way, but no - Dear God No - the shelter had disappeared, and in its place was a smoking pile of rubble. It hadn't just disintegrated, it had disappeared, and all those poor souls with it. Only a few moments earlier I had watched them rushing to oblivion.

By now I had had a lot of experience of bomb incidents, but this one got to me. This time it was up close and personal, I started to shake, and my legs refused to function. I wanted to run to help but I couldn't move. What help could I give anyway? They were all beyond any terrestrial help.

Eventually I managed to stagger to my feet and I reached the spot where the shelter stood. .... I will spare you the rest.

The war dragged on and we managed as best as we could, on the home front it was a time of young men like me, and old men like dad, and women - God bless 'em. The women at work became essential to maintain the factories, the services, and the land.

The Women's Land Army was formed to provide a labour force for farmers wherever it was needed. And the Land Girls, as they were known, became absolutely essential in the fight to provide food. They were mostly young women, and they really looked smart in their uniforms of dark green jumper, over a yellow shirt, with brown jodhpurs worn with long socks, shoes or wellies.

I met one Land Girl on a visit to Higham's Park Lake, and she was a cracker: Chestnut hair, deep brown eyes, and with a super figure, her name was Christine. I managed to see Christine often until she was sent away, and we spent quite a bit of time together, mostly in and around Epping Forest, and outside the pubs in the summertime. Happy memories!

Everywhere economy was the byword, 'Make do and mend', 'Dig for victory', 'Sew and Save', 'What mothers can do to save buying new' etc., 'War-time economy this ...', and 'War-time economy that ...' Pamphlets everywhere and posters on every hoarding.

The Board of Trade issued little booklets from time to time. In these a 'Mrs. Sew & Sew' would advise housewives on many varied subjects such as, 'How to Patch Elbows and Trousers' or 'How to Patch Sheets and Blankets' 'How to Patch Shirts and Turn Collars', and so on.

'Good Gawd Nellie, they'll be tellin' us 'ow t' darn socks next. Wot a waste o paper.'

It was decreed that aluminium saucepans were to be requisitioned to make aircraft:

'They can't have mine, what will I cook me old man's dinner in? I aint got nuffink else.'

'You can 'ave one o mind Ethel, I've got a couple of spare enamel ones.'
And so we managed, with everyone helping each other as best we could. Basically if you didn't help each other - there was no help at all.

Our park railings and garden gates were melted down for ammunitions, bones were collected to make glue for Spitfires, and all paper was recycled. Kitchen waste, what there was of it, was collected for pig swill, nothing was wasted. Even my drawing pencils came without their usual coat of glossy paint, and the utility mark of a filled in three quarter circle, was on everything.

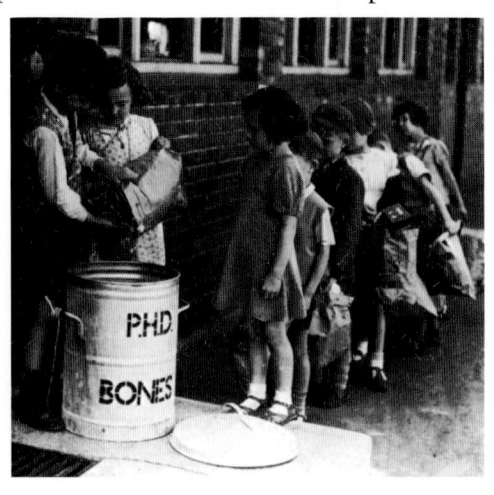

P.H.D.? Public Health Department.

Woollens were un-picked and re-knitted. Paper was used both sides, and gummed labels could be obtained, free of charge from the Post Office, for the re-use of envelopes.

To be strictly honest, not all paper was used both sides. I remember Dad brought home a toilet roll once, it had Hitler's face printed on every sheet.

An official notice read; 'Warning'. Any person burning or destroying wastepaper is guilty of an offence against the National War Effort.'

It was difficult to comply with that 100% of course, but we did our best. Perhaps the greatest waste of paper was the issue of so many pointless pamphlets by government departments. For instance one read
'Food is a munition of war, don't waste it.' – as if we would.
And another gem said;
'Look out in the Blackout.' Now that was really helpful!
The Ministry of Food issued a handbill that told us to -
'Eat more vegetables'
Very pointless advice with the meat ration 12ozs. (340grams) per week.
And how about this priceless offering? -
'Don't risk your life in the blackout - Stay indoors if you can.'

There was a Black Market trade in anything scarce, and everything was, so the Spivs, or Wide Boys, as we called them, would sell you almost anything - at a price.

The famous cartoon character Chad, looked over a wall, and made us smile with his captions of 'Wot no bananas' or whatever else was unobtainable, like nylon stockings for example.

He had plenty of material to poke fun at.

A Banana was the embodiment of everything scarce, since from the early days of the war, bananas were completely unobtainable.
By Government decree, they were not to be imported as they were inefficient in food value compared to the space required in a ship's hold.

I bred rabbits in our back yard in rows of wire fronted boxes, those that we didn't eat, I sold or traded. Dad kept chickens and worked on his allotment. Mum worked wonders with very little, and somehow we managed. Mum got free orange juice for the baby, and Sis got into trouble for drinking it, so did I if I got caught.

We did our best to keep everything as normal as possible, it was good for our moral anyway, and in November 1941 or 2, a local paper shop discovered a stock of old fireworks. So we made a guy and we had our Guy Fawkes night as usual, well, not quite as usual as we couldn't light the bonfire at night, so we burnt him in the afternoon and we let off a few fireworks.

Iris was now married, and her husband was home on leave. He gave me two Vary Light Flares which he had 'borrowed', but how to set them off without a proper pistol? I clamped one in my bench vice, and with the now proven 'poker and hammer technique' off it went. Alas without the correct firing mechanism, it didn't go very far upward. Not very far at all in truth, just high enough to reach next door's roof and to lodge in the gutter where it burned in a fuming magnesium red for several minutes. Fortunately plastic guttering was not in use then and the gutter was made of cast iron, so no harm was done, except to my right ear when Mum's heavy hand landed on it.

I reached the age of eighteen in 1942 and became due for call-up, I was a minor part of a design team working on advanced bombsights then, my firm registered me as being on *Work of National Importance*, and so my enlistment into the forces was deferred for a while.

Folks *back home* could send cigarettes out to troops overseas, duty free. Players, Gold Flake, and Craven 'A' cost 3s9d (19p) for 120. and Woodbines, Weights and Tenners were sent for 3s4d (17.p) for 150. But in *civy street* cigarettes became difficult to obtain, and supplies went *under the counter*, reserved and available to regulars only.

The pilot-less flying bombs started in the summer of 1944. The first one landed in London on the 13th June. They were quickly nicknamed Doodlebugs, but they were officially known as V1s as soon as the V2 rockets started to arrive.

On one fine Saturday afternoon I was sticking a notice on John's shop window, when we heard the familiar drone, the engine cut, then that awful silence as we waited for the bomb to land. It fell on a crowded double-decker bus in Hoe Street, between the station and High Street. I was close by, and even in the shop doorway I was knocked over by the blast. I ran up the road to the scene to help. Glass and devastation was everywhere, rubble, pieces of bus, pieces of bodies, small fires, silence and dust confronted me. Not a thing moved; it was as if time itself was frozen. The scene is etched in my mind, mostly the eerie silence, broken only by a low sobbing. The effects of blast can be inexplicable, one young woman stood within twenty yards of the explosion. She was in deep shock but otherwise unharmed, incredibly the blast had removed all of her clothes except her shoes. It was as if she had undressed herself, she was covered only in a fine grey dust.

I still don't understand how a blast can do that, but I know that it did. I put my coat around her and carried her to an ambulance that had just arrived, kindly hands took care of her and my last image was as she boarded the ambulance wrapped in a red blanket.

I remember working there until well after dark, the carnage I was used to by this time, but the details are too gruesome to contemplate.

The first of the V2 rockets fell at Chiswick, south of the Thames on the 8th. Sept.1944

The war with Germany eventually ended with VE Day on 8th.May 1945.

But Japan fought on until the Atom bombs ended it on VJ Day on the 14th. August 1945.

The official Victory Celebrations didn't take place until the 8th.June 1946.

Even after the war ended with Germany we queued for everything, even rationed items were scarce and often the full ration was not available in the shops. Bread was still on ration well into 1946. It was reported that every housewife spent, on average, one hour per day queuing for something

In May 1945 Street parties and miles of streamers and bunting, celebrated the end of the German conflict. But after that had been cleared away and the dust had settled, we had to face the reality of what was left.

Our family had been extremely lucky. None of our relations had been killed, and we all had our homes still standing, but everywhere people struggled to maintain and rebuild a life of some sort. Now was the time when a community spirit and individual resolve would really be put to the test.

I was now 21, where had my youth gone? I had finally grown up.
I had become a fully qualified Engineering Draughtsman and on my way to becoming a designer, or an 'Inventor', as I would have said ten years ago.

I was eventually conscripted into the army in 1946 and served in The Royal Electrical and Mechanical Engineers. (R.E.M.E.) Here, after my initial training, I was given an unexpected nine months full time course in electronics. This proved to be an invaluable addition to my other qualifications, and I have never ceased to be grateful to the Army for that additional tuition.

Hence, as a qualified R.E.M.E. Radar Technician, I was posted to an A.T.S. training camp for women radar operators, and my job, with five others, was to repair and maintain the radar equipment. The six of us were billeted inside a camp of 300 young women, in the middle of nowhere.
In a place called Washington, in County Durham, to be exact. With 300 wonderful girls of Unit 597, and I wasn't married then either - phew.
Local Army camps would invite *our* girls when they put on a dance, and so we went along too. After the dance, the girls were shepherded by the MPs back to the Bedford trucks to take them back to camp. The local Army lads tried to board as well for obvious reasons, but the MPs would have none of that. But we six - we belonged - we wore the flashes of the 597 Unit. When the girls called from the back of the truck 'Come on Alby darling', and we climbed aboard, the other Army lads could be seen going green with envy. And so they might, as that was the most delightful posting that anyone ever devised for a young single man of 22. I learned a lot from the Army.

After that posting I went home on leave (To recover I guess.) Not much to do in *civy street* when all of your mates are away. On the Saturday evening Dad had organised one of his Church Socials, so with nothing better to do I went along. I only remember noticing one other person there, a very attractive A.T.S. sergeant. It turned out that she was only there for the same reason as me, because her mum was playing the piano for the social, and she had nothing better to do.
Correspondence led to us getting married in June 1947. And that happy union lasted for forty years until August 1987, when she died of Altzheimers Disease.

Her wedding dress was made from a German parachute; nylon I think, but it looked like silk, it was a very beautiful ivory material. We spent our honeymoon on the Norfolk Broads with one gallon of fuel for the engine. We didn't see much of the Broads.

Princess Elizabeth and The Duke of Edinburgh were also married in

1947. It was reported that the princess was given an extra 100 clothing coupons for her wedding clothes.

We weren't, but I much preferred the parachute silk and its contents.

I made my own television set in 1948 using a nine inch radar tube and ex-service parts. Television transmissions had resumed by the end of 1946. Our flickering green image was a source of wonder and a novelty that greatly increased our popularity with the neighbours.

When I left the Army in 1948 I was given a green National Identity Card (which I still have) and I was lucky enough to get employment as a designer draughtsman with a famous Radio and Television manufacturer, at the princely salary of £34 per month.

I achieved my first Directorship in 1962, my second with an electronics company in 1967, and my third as a Design Director, started in 1970 from which I retired at the age of 62 in 1986.

Looking back, it has been a good life, full of happiness and achievement, and although this book only embraces the first 28% of my life so far, the rest - as they say - is another story.

Long may it continue.

In 1992 I met, and married, my present wife Barbara
– God bless her –
I dedicate this book to her in thanks
for her loving support and indulgence.

That's it – I do hope that you have enjoyed my reminiscences. Fortunately I found in writing, that the memories of my early years remain more vividly in my mind that those of the years in between. Perhaps this is because the young mind is less selective in what it chooses to retain, and in later years we only remember what we think is important.

I now have the satisfaction of knowing that I have made a record, should the years to come afflict me with a degree of dementia. Now I can answer my Grandchildren when they ask 'What was it like Grandad when ... ... ?

May your God watch over you.

Alby G. White ©*2002.*

COINS OF THE REALM
~ In everyday use before 1972 ~

FARTHING   4 = 1 Penny
0.1p decimal   960 = 1 Pound

HALFPENNY   2 = 1 Penny
0.2p decimal   480 = 1 Pound

PENNY   12 = 1 Shilling
0.4p decimal   240 = 1 Pound

The Penny, Halfpenny, and Farthing were all made of copper with a little brass added to made them harder.

THREE PENNY PIECE *1.25p*
Made of Bronze and called a JOEY

THREE PENNY PIECE *1.25p*
Made of pure Silver.

SIXPENCE   *2.5p decimal*
Made of Silver and later of Cupro-nickel.   Always called a TANNER

SHILLING   *5p*   20 = 1 Pound
Always called a BOB

FLORIN   *10p*   10 = 1 Pound
Known as TWO BOB.
All the early silver coins were made of pure Silver & gradually replaced by ones made of Cupro-nickel. The Florin was the last one replaced.

HALFCROWN = Two shillings and sixpence. Called a half Dollar because a full Crown equalled an American Dollar in value.
A CROWN = Five shillings, but was little used because it was too heavy

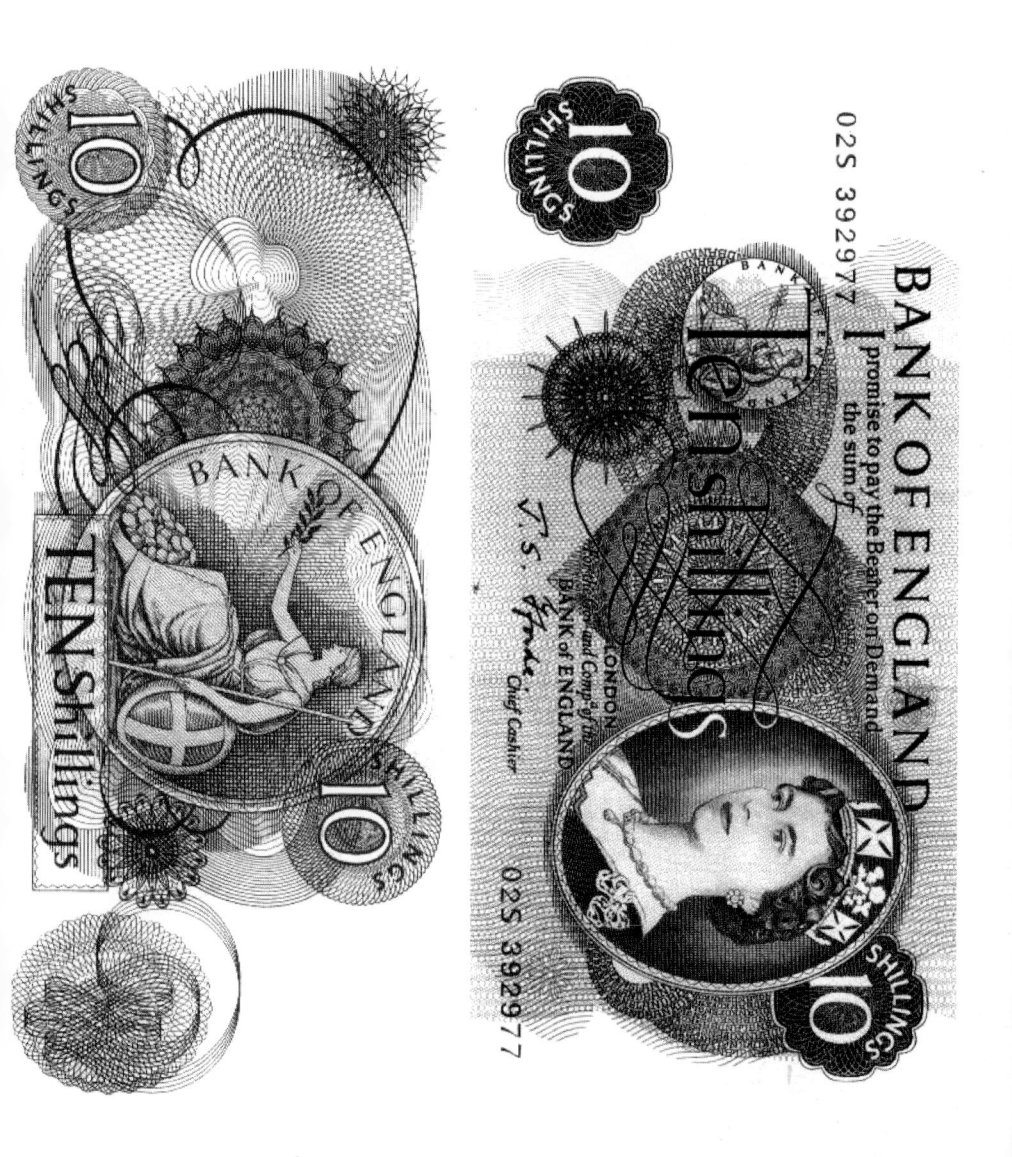

The TEN SHILLING NOTE, (or Ten Bob Note) shown here actual size, was printed in one colour, Brown on an ivory coloured paper.
The only anti-counterfeit device was a single silver strip inserted across the note, between the letters L and A of ENGLAND.

THE POUND STERLING shown here actual size, was printed in shades of Green on ivory paper. A silver strip ran across the note through the a in Bank. The Obverse side was also mainly Green with shades of Pink in the centre, and Blue at the edges.